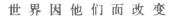

世界因他们而改变

特斯拉自传

| 中英双语版 |

[美]尼古拉·特斯拉◎著

师文慧◎译

中国科学技术出版社

·北 京·

图书在版编目（CIP）数据

特斯拉自传：汉、英 /（美）尼古拉·特斯拉著；师文慧译 . —北京：中国科学技术出版社，2023.5

书名原文：My Inventions

ISBN 978-7-5236-0164-8

I. ①特… II. ①尼… ②师… III. ①特斯拉（Tesla, Nikola 1856—1943）–自传 IV. ① K837.126.1

中国国家版本馆 CIP 数据核字（2023）第 075634 号

策划编辑	周少敏　郭秋霞　崔家岭
责任编辑	郭秋霞　崔家岭
装帧设计	中文天地
责任校对	凌　雪
责任印制	马宇晨

出　　版	中国科学技术出版社
发　　行	中国科学技术出版社有限公司发行部
地　　址	北京市海淀区中关村南大街16号
邮　　编	100081
发行电话	010-62173865
传　　真	010-62173081
网　　址	http://www.cspbooks.com.cn

开　　本	787mm×1092mm　1/32
字　　数	119千字
印　　张	7.75
版　　次	2023年5月第1版
印　　次	2023年5月第1次印刷
印　　刷	北京长宁印刷有限公司
书　　号	ISBN 978-7-5236-0164-8 / K・362
定　　价	58.00元

目 录

Contents

第一章

少年时代

很大程度上，人类的进步依赖于发明，这是创造性思维最重要的产物。发明的最终目的，是完全掌握物质世界的规律，驾驭自然的力量，更大程度地满足人类的需求。这项艰巨工作经常被误解，还可能会徒劳无功。然而，发明家会在令人愉悦的发明过程中得到满足，并且知道自己属于那个特别人群中的一员。没有这群特别的人，人类早就在与大自然残酷的斗争中灭亡了。

就我自己而言，我已经对发明过程中带来的这种美妙享受感到无比快乐，以至于多年来生活中的其他快乐与之相比都会黯然失色。大家认为我是世界上最勤奋的

---

* 为方便阅读，译者为一些段落添加了标题。

人之一。如果思考也算是劳动，那么我当之无愧，因为我几乎所有醒着的时间都致力于此；但如果工作以按照庸俗的、严格的某种规则，考核我在特定时间内能干多少活，那我可能就是一个游手好闲之辈。我认为，如果强迫自己做不喜欢的事，每一次努力都是在耗费生命的能量，直到油尽灯枯。幸运的是，我从来没有付出过这样的代价，我在做自己喜欢的事情中实现了生命的价值。

我把自己的回忆写成一系列文章，在《电气实验员》编辑的协助下发表。这些文章主要是针对年轻的男性读者。虽然我不情愿详述年轻时的情况，也不怎么愿意讲对我的职业生涯起决定性作用的环境和事件，但既然要写，我还是尽可能忠实地还原事实。

人类最初的尝试纯属本能，生动而随意的想象会自然激发。随着年龄的增长，理性逐渐占主导地位，我们变得越来越刻意，越来越有计划。然而，那些早期的冲动才是人生的重要时刻，虽然不会立即产生效果，却会塑造我们的命运。的确，我现在觉得，如果我及时理解、顺应这些冲动，而不是压制它们，我想我能留给世界更多有价值的东西。遗憾的是，直到成年后，我才意识到自己原来是一个发明家。

家庭影响

这是由多种原因造成的。首先，我有一个哥哥，他天赋非凡——当时的生物学研究也无法解释这种罕见的现象。但他在一次骑马时出现意外，不幸夭折，使我的父母悲痛万分。这匹马是一位好朋友赠送给我们的一匹好马，阿拉伯品种，外形俊朗，颇通人性，受到全家人喜爱。这匹马对我父亲有救命之恩。那是一个冬天的雪夜，我父亲骑马赶路，行至荒山野岭之处遇到了狼群！马儿受到狼群侵扰，惊吓之中把我父亲猛地摔在地上。但马儿颇通人性，引群狼远远离开我父亲。在摆脱狼群后，马儿全身是血，精疲力竭地回家报信。报信之后，马儿又立即奔赴现场去救我父亲。家人、朋友组成的搜救队被马儿远远地甩在后面。在搜救队离出事地点还有相当长的距离时，我父亲骑着马迎面而来！原来，在马儿返回时，我父亲已经恢复了意识，他重新上马赶路，完全没有意识到自己已经在雪地里躺了几个小时。就是这匹救过我父亲的马，在一次意外中使我哥哥受了伤，他后因伤势过重而亡。我亲眼目睹了这悲惨一幕，尽管已经过去了半个多世纪，往日之情景犹在眼前。相比我哥哥的天资与成就，我的努力都显得微不足道。

在我看来，我所做的任何值得称道的事情，只会让我的父母更加强烈地感受到他们失去我哥哥的痛苦。受此影响，我从小就对自己缺乏信心。但是，让我至今记忆犹新的事件表明，我并不是一个笨小孩。有一天，我在街上和小伙伴们玩耍，一群市议员们正要穿街而过。这些可敬的绅士中最年长的一位富翁停下来给我们每个人一枚银币。当他走到我跟前，突然停下来命令道："看着我的眼睛。"我迎着他的目光，伸手去接那枚价值不菲的硬币。但令我沮丧的是，他说："不，你太聪明了，这枚硬币微不足道，对你没有用！"

长辈们曾经讲过一件我小时候的趣事。我有两位姑妈，满脸皱纹，其中一位长着两颗像大象獠牙一样突出的大龅牙，每次亲我时她都会把它埋在我的脸颊上。她给我的深情拥抱乏味之极，让我胆战心惊。有一次我被妈妈抱在怀里，两位姑妈问我她俩谁更漂亮。我仔细打量她们的脸，若有所思地指着其中一个人回答道："你比不上她丑。"

让我不够自信还有一个原因。我刚出生时，家里就想让我子承父业，这使我烦恼无比。我渴望成为一名工程师，但我父亲坚决反对。我爷爷，曾是在拿破仑军队服役的军官；我的伯伯，是一家著名机构的数学教授。受爷爷影响，伯伯与父亲都接受过军事教育。但让人匪夷所思的是，父亲选择神职人员为他的职业，并取得了显赫地位。他博学多才，是名副其实的自然哲学家、诗人和作家。据说，他的布道与亚伯拉罕·阿·圣克拉拉[1]的布道一样雄辩有力。他的记忆力惊人，经常背诵好几种语言的作品。他经常开玩笑地说，如果一些经典丢失了，他可以重新写出它们。他的写作风格备受推崇。他的句子短而精，充满机智和讽刺。他的话总是诙谐幽默，语出惊人。举两个例子可以证明。

我们农场有个工人叫马内，是个"斗鸡眼"。有一

特斯拉的父亲米卢廷·特斯拉，是斯米连村的东正教会牧师。

---

[1] 亚伯拉罕·阿·圣克拉拉（Abraham a Sancta-Clara），1644—1709，曾任奥地利的宫廷神父，他的布道非常雄辩、幽默，富有感染力，吸引了大量听众，他写的布道小册子也非常流行。

天，他正在挥动斧头劈柴，我父亲就站在附近。因为是斜视，所以父亲觉得马内正盯着他看，好像下一秒斧子就抡到他的头上一样。所以，父亲就警告马内说："看在上帝的份上，马内，不要劈你正在看的，而要劈你打算劈的东西！"还有一次，他与朋友们开车出去兜风。其中一个朋友不小心把他那件名贵的皮大衣碰在了车轮上。我父亲提醒他说："当心你的大衣，别弄脏了我的轮胎。"他有一个自言自语的奇怪习惯，并且经常一个人分饰多个角色、声情并茂地对话，还自己和自己发生激烈的争论。不同的角色不同的语气，惟妙惟肖。不知情的人走到门外，一定会以为房间里有好几个人在吵架。

虽然我确认我的创造力是来自母亲的影响，但父亲对我的训练也起了很大的作用。这些训练五花八门。例如，猜测对方的想法，发现一些表达形式的缺陷，重复长句子或进行心算。这些日常课程旨在增强记忆力和推理能力，尤其是培养批判性意识。这对我的创造力的培养无疑是非常有益的。

我的母亲出身于本国最古老的家族，同时还是一个发明世家，我的外公、曾外公都发明了许多家用工具、农业工具和其他用途的工具。我母亲是一位真正伟大的女性，拥有罕见的技巧、勇气和毅力。她勇敢地面对生活的狂风暴雨，经历过许多艰难的时刻。当她十六岁时，一场致命的瘟疫席卷了整个国家。外祖父被请去为垂死的人做最后的圣餐礼，而我母亲独自去帮助一位患有可怕疾病的邻居。这个家庭里面所有的成员，共五个人，都接二连三地死去。母亲为遗体清洗、穿衣和停放，并按照当地的习俗用鲜花装饰在遗体的周围。当外祖父赶来时，他发现一切都准备妥当，可以直接举行基督徒的葬礼。我的母亲是顶级的发明家。我相信，如果没有远离现代生活及其各种"机遇"，她会取得更大的成就。她发明并制造了各式各样的工具和设备，并用她纺出的线编织出精美的图案。她还亲自种植植物并获取纤维。从早到晚，她孜孜不倦地工作，家里的衣着摆设，大多是她手工制作的。六十多岁的时候，母亲的手指还很灵活，就算在睫毛上打三个结也不在话下。

逼真的幻象

我开悟晚还有另一个更重要的原因。

小时候，我眼前经常会出现奇特的幻象，幻象中常常伴随着强烈的闪光。这让我看不清真实的景物，干扰了我的思想和行动。这些幻象的内容并不是我想象的东西，而是我真正见过的事物和场景。比如，当我听到一个词时，它所对应的形象会栩栩如生地呈现在我的眼前。真正的问题在于，有些时候我完全无法区分我所看到的究竟是实物还是幻象！这给我带来了极大的不适和焦虑。在我咨询过的心理学或生理学专家中，没有一个能令人满意地解释我这个情况。因为别人都没有遇到过这种情况，就是我遇到了——虽然我觉得我哥哥在世时也可能遇到了类似的麻烦。我提出的理论是，这些图像是大脑在高度兴奋下在视网膜上产生的反射作用，而不是因为病和痛苦而产生的错乱，因为在其他方面我没有什么问题。为了说明这给我带来多大的麻烦，我举个例子。假设我亲眼目睹了一场葬礼或某种令人伤心的场面，然后，不可避免地，在夜深人静之时，一幅生动的画面会突然出现在我的眼前！无论我多么竭尽全力驱赶它，但它岿然不动，依然如故。我用手推它也无济于事，它甚至会固定悬浮在天空之中。如果我的解释是正确的，即大脑可以把影像投在视网膜上，那么通过某种技术，大脑应该能够将人们构想的任何物体的图像投射到屏幕上并使其可见。这样的进步将彻底改变所有人际关系。我深信，这个奇迹能够而且将会在未来实现。补充一点，实际上我花了很多心思来解决这个问题。

为了摆脱这些折磨人或有些恐怖的幻象，我试图将注意力集中在我所看到的其他事情上，这样我就可以暂时得到解脱。但是，这需要我不断地创造出新的场景。不久之后，我发现自己已经用尽了能用的所有图像。我的"图像卷轴"已经用完了，因为我看到的只是这个世界的很小一部分——头脑中只有我家和周围环境中的东西。当我第二次或第三次进行这些心理操作，驱逐我视野中的恐怖幻象时，这个"药方"就失效了。然后，我本能地开始在我所知道的小世界的范围之外进行"远足"，我"看到"了新的场景。这些新场景起初非常模糊，并且会飘忽不定。当我试图把注意力集中在它们身上时，它们就不见了，但渐渐地，我成功地修复了它们。这些幻象获得了力量和独特性，最终呈现出与真实事物一样的细枝末节。我很快发现，只要在自己的视野中走向远方，就能不断获得新的景物，收获满满，所以我开始旅行——当然是在我的脑海里！每天晚上（有时是白天），当我独自一人时，会开始我的旅程——去新的地方、城市和国家，在那里生活，结识新朋友。尽管难以置信，但事实是他们对我来说就像现实生活中的那些人一样值得珍惜。对我而言，他们如在眼前，与真实的人没有什么两样。

我一直这样做，直到差不多17岁时，才开始认真地转向发明。随后，我高兴地发现，把设想转为具体的形象对我来说轻而易举。不需要模型，不需要图，也不需要实验，我可以在脑海中把它们都想象成真实的。因此，我在不知不觉中被引导，发展出一种我认为将创造性概念和想法具体化的新方法。它与纯粹的实验完全相反，并且在我看来更加迅速和有效。当一个人制造出一台装置，以将一个粗略的想法付诸实践时，他会发现自己不可避免地会陷入该装置的细节和缺陷之中。当他继续改进和重建时，他的专注力会减弱，逐渐忘记自己的初心。这样一来，他虽然可以勉强实现目标，但总是效果不佳。

我的方法不一样。我不急于付诸实施。当我有一个想法时，我会立即开始在我的想象中构建它。我在脑海中改变结构，进行预演，改进并操作设备。把涡轮机放在脑海中运行与厂房中对其进行测试，对我来说没有什么区别。如果设计上有问题，我就能发现其中的细节。通过这种方式，我能够在不借助实物的情况下快速发展和完善一个概念。当我把能想到的所有可能的改进都体现在发明中，并且消灭所有缺陷时，我才将其付诸实践。二十年来，我通过想象设计出的设备，在实际上执行起来与想象中并无偏差，无一例外。为什么我可以做到这一点呢？因为无论工程、电气和机械，还是其他学科，它们都使用数学的方法来逻辑推理。只要根据现有的理论和已知数据进行严密的推理，就能推出正确的结果。我认为，如果有人将一个粗略的想法付诸实践，只不过是在浪费精力、金钱和时间！

除此之外，我早期的痛苦还得到了另一种补偿。不断的脑力劳动锻炼了我的观察力，使我发现了一个非常重要的事实。我注意到幻象都是对之前特殊条件下实际场景的再现和加工，我就强迫自己在幻象与实际场景之间建立联系。过了一段时间，这种联系就会自动完成，我在连接因果关系方面获得了极大的便利。很快，令我惊讶的是，我意识到自己的每一个想法都是由外部印象暗示的。不仅如此，我所有的动作都是以类似的方式提示的。随着时间的推移，我完全明白我只是一个有运动能力的机器人，对感觉器官的刺激做出反应，并据此思考和行动。依靠这种模式，我实际上的收获是远程自动控制的技术，到目前为止，它的运行不算完美。然而，我相信，它的潜在可能性最终会实现。多年来，我一直在设计自动控制机，并坚信可以创造出在一定程度上具有智能的机制，并将在许多商业和工业部门中引发一场革命。

大约 12 岁的时候，我第一次通过有意识的努力成功地从我的幻象中消除了一个自己不想见到的图像，但我却对上面提到的闪光仍然无能为力。这些闪光或许是我经历中最奇怪的东西，它们通常发生在我发现自己处于危险或痛苦的境地，或者当我非常兴奋时。有些时候，我能看到我周围的所有空气都充满了跳动的红色火焰。这种幻象的强度不是在减弱，而是随着时间的推移而增加，在大约 25 岁时达到了最大值。1883 年，我在巴黎时，一家著名的法国制造商向我发出了参加射击探险的邀请，我接受了。我长期在工厂之中，野外新鲜的空气对我产生了奇妙的提神作用。那天晚上我回到城市时，有一种真真切切的感觉——我的大脑着火了。脑海中一个小太阳在熊熊燃烧，我整晚都在对我受折磨的头部进行冷敷。最终，闪光的频率和强度都减弱了，但仍然过了三周多才完全平息。当这家制造商再次向我发出邀请时，我的回答是：坚决不去！

当我突然有些新想法或新发现时，这些闪光的幻象仍然时不时地出现，但它们的强度比之前小，不再令人兴奋不安。当闭上眼睛时，我总是首先观察到一个非常暗而均匀的蓝色背景，与晴朗但没有星星的夜晚天空差不多。几秒钟后，这个领域变得活跃起来，无数闪烁的绿色薄片排列成几层，朝着我前进。然后，在右边背景上出现了一个美丽的图案，由两个平行且相距很近的线条组成，彼此成直角，颜色各异，以黄绿色和金色为主。紧接着，线条变得更加明亮，整体上密密麻麻地散布着金星并闪烁着光芒。这张照片在视野中缓慢移动，大约十秒钟后消失在左侧，留下一片相当不愉快和沉闷的灰色地面，但很快就让位于汹涌的云海，似乎试图将自己塑造成活生生的形状。奇怪的是，在达到第二阶段之前，我无法将任何形状投射到这种灰色中。每次在入睡之前，人或物体的图像都会从我的视野中掠过。当我看到他们时，我知道自己即将失去意识。如果他们不来，那就意味着一个不眠之夜。

我可以用另一种奇怪的经历来说明想象力在我早年的生活中发挥了多大的作用。像大多数孩子一样，我喜欢跳跃，并产生了一种在空中飘浮的强烈愿望。偶尔从山上吹来一股清新的强风，让我的身体像软木塞一样轻盈，感觉自己在空中跳跃和漂浮很长一段时间，这是一种令人愉快的感觉。后来知道这不过是想象之后，我感到非常失望。

　　在那期间，我养成了许多奇怪的好恶和习惯，其中一些可以认为是外部原因，而另一些则莫名其妙。我对女性的耳环有强烈的反感，但对其他饰品，如手镯，根据其设计样式，或多或少会感到满意。看到一颗珍珠几乎会让我心旷神怡，而水晶或具有棱角的闪闪发光的物体会让我着迷。我从不碰别人的头发，除非是用左轮手枪抵着我的头。我会因为看到一只桃子而发烧，会因为嗅到樟脑丸的味道而难受。即使是现在，我对这类的事情也无法置之不理。当我将小纸片放入盛满液体的盘子中时，我总能感觉到嘴里有一种奇怪而可怕的味道。我走路的时候必须数着步数，喝汤、喝咖啡时得计算喝了多少——不这样我就很难受。如果我要做重复的动作或操作，其次数必须能被三整除。如果我不小心弄错了，得重新来一遍，即使这需要花费几个小时。

意志的觉醒

一直到八岁，我的性格都很软弱，而且优柔寡断。我既没有勇气也没有力量下定决心去做一件事情。我的情绪如大海的波浪，上下起伏，相当不稳定。为了实现愿望，我的精力就像九头蛇的头一样，成倍增加。然而，我被生死所困，痛苦万分；我被宗教所扰，忧虑害怕；我被幻觉所左右，徘徊在魔鬼、鬼魂、食人魔和其他邪恶的黑暗怪物的恐惧之中。然后，突然之间，发生了巨大的变化，我的人生从此与之前不同了。万物之中，图书是我的最爱。父亲有一个很大的藏书间，我总是千方百计地溜进去读书。但是，匪夷所思的是，父亲不允许我读书，一旦发现就会大发雷霆。当他发现我在偷偷看书时，就把蜡烛藏起来了。可能是他不想让阅读影响到我的视力。但我得到了牛油，制作了灯芯，用锡纸当容器，一盏简易灯就做好了。每天晚上，我都会堵住钥匙孔和门缝以免光线引起父亲的注意，然后通宵达旦地看书。东方发白时，其他人仍在睡梦之中，只有母亲开始了她一天繁忙的工作。有一次，我偶然看到一本名为《奥鲍菲：奥鲍之子》的小说，这是匈牙利著名作家米克洛什·约希卡的塞尔维亚语译本。这项工作以某种方式唤醒了我沉睡的意志力，我开始练习自我控制。起初，我的决心像春天的雪迅速消融，但过了一阵子，我就克服了自己的弱点，这让我感到了一种前所未有的快乐——我能轻松地依靠意志做事情了。随着时间的推移，这种剧烈的脑力锻炼成为我的第二天性。一开始我的愿望必须被意志抑制，但逐渐地愿望和意志就合二为一了。经过多年这样的训练，我收放自如，完全驾驭了自己。有些不良嗜好让意志最坚强的人也无法摆脱，但对我来说易如反掌。比如，到了一定年龄，我染上了赌博之习，这让我的父母非常担心。坐下来打牌开赌对我来说是快乐的源泉。我父亲过着模范的生活，不能原谅我沉迷于赌博，无谓地浪费时间和金钱。我意志很强大，但理念很糟糕。我对他说："戒掉赌瘾对我来说是小菜一碟，可是我在赌博中获得天堂般的快乐，为何要戒呢？"这样一来，我父亲经常发泄他对我的愤怒和蔑视，这一点与我母亲大不相同。我的母亲了解男人，她知道一个男人能否得到救赎只能靠自己的努力。我记得，有一天下午，当我输光了所有的钱，还想再赌一注时，我母亲送来一卷钞票："去享受吧！早败家，早醒悟，我相信你。"母亲做得很对，我瞬间就征服自我。太轻松了，我觉得这赌瘾还是不够大，如果再强烈一百倍，我仍然可以轻松戒除，那样就更能显示我无与伦比的意志力了。我不仅战胜了它，还把它从心里彻底清除，不留一丝痕迹。从那时起，我对任何形式的赌博都漠不关心，就像拔牙，连根拔除。

在另一个时期，我抽烟非常凶，以致健康受到了严重的威胁。然后我用意志战胜了欲望，不仅停止了抽烟，而且完全戒掉了。之前我有心脏病，直到我判断这可能与我每天早上喝一杯咖啡有关时，我立即停止了。但我承认这不是一件容易的事。通过这种方式，我停止并抑制了其他不良习惯和欲望，这不仅保护了我的生命，而且因能完成大多数人无法完成的事情而获得了巨大的满足感。

在格拉茨理工学院和布拉格大学完成学业后，我的精神完全崩溃了。在此期间，在我身上发生了许多奇怪和难以置信的现象。

第二章

步入发明之门

　　我将简要介绍这些非凡的经历，因为它们可能会引起心理学和生理学研究者的兴趣。也因为这段痛苦的时期，对我的心理状况及随后的工作产生了极大的影响。但是，我必须首先将之前的情况和条件做一个梳理，并尽量弄清其中的来龙去脉。

内省的力量

　　从小我就被迫"三省吾身"，这给我带来了很多痛苦。但现在看来，这是因祸得福。这让我认识到，内省不但在保护生命方面有不可估量的价值，还是一种成就人生的手段。职业的压力，各种各样繁杂的信息，源源不断地涌向我们的意识，很容易让我们在不知不觉中步入危险境地。大多数人都沉浸在对外部世界的沉思中，以至于他们完全忘记了他们自己身体内部正在发生的事情。

数百万人的过早死亡主要可以追溯到这个原因。即使在那些谨慎行事的人中，也会犯这种错误：忽略了实际的危险，却去消除想象中的危险。一个人的情况也或多或少地适用于整个民族。例如，禁酒运动。这个国家现在正在采取非常严厉的措施禁止饮酒。其实，一个确定的事实是：咖啡、茶叶、烟草、口香糖这类食品的放任，特别是对低龄人群的不加限制，才是对国民最大的伤害。例如，在我还是学生的时候，我从咖啡之乡维也纳出版的资料中得出结论，死于心脏病的人有时会达到死亡总数的 67%。我猜测，类似的观察结果可能会出现在茶叶消费过度的城市。这些美味的饮料令人过于兴奋并逐渐耗尽大脑的神经网络，还严重干扰血液循环。因为它们的伤害影响缓慢且不易察觉，应该更加谨慎地享用。另一方面，烟草虽然使思考变得轻松，但很可能会减损智力中原有的专注力，而这些专注力是原创和生机勃勃的智力活动所必需的。口香糖在短时间内有帮助，但很快就会耗尽腺体系统的分泌，更不用说它引起的副作用了。少量的酒精的摄入会有些益处，但大量吸收时会产生毒性。至于它是作为威士忌摄入还是在胃中由糖产生的没有什么区别。不容忽视的是，这正是大自然适者生存的严厉法则，不适应法则的人会被淘汰。热心的改革者还应该注意，因为人类与生俱来的任性，采用宽松的"顺其自然"的态度比用强制手段更为可取。

事实上，虽然我们需要某些食物的刺激才能在当前的生活条件下呈现最好的状态，但我们必须保持节制，在各个方面控制我们的食欲和嗜好。节制是我多年来一直在做的事情，以此让自己在身心上保持年轻。节制并非总是为我所好，但我已经在创造的愉快经历中得到了充足的回报。为了让一些人能相信我的戒律和信念，我来回忆一两个例子。

不久前，一个寒冷的夜晚，地面湿滑，我没有找到出租车，只得步行回酒店。在我身后差不多半个街区的地方，有一个男人，也像我一样步履匆匆。突然，我意念一动，脑海中有一道亮光划过！神经有反应，肌肉绷紧，双腿发力，腾空而起，在空中翻转一百八十度，头下脚上，用手撑地，随即恢复正常，继续赶路，似乎什么都没有发生过。我这番操作惊呆了后面的陌生人。他追上我时，我继续走路，就当什么事也没发生。"您今年多大？"他审慎地打量着我，问道。"哦，算是五十九岁吧，"我回答说，"怎么啦？""嗯，"他说，"我见过猫这样做，但从来没有见人这样做过。"大约一个月后，我想订制一副新眼镜，去找眼科医生。他让我进行一项常规视力测试。当我在相当远的距离还能轻松看到视力表上最小的字母时，他难以置信地看着我。当我告诉他我已经年近六旬时，他更是惊讶地倒吸了一口凉气。我的朋友经常说我的西装就像手套一样合身，但他们不知道我所有的衣服都是按照 35 年前的尺寸制作的，从未改变过。35 年来，我的体重没有增加一磅，也没有减少一磅。

在这方面，我可以讲一个有趣的故事。1885 年冬天的一天晚上，托马斯·爱迪生先生、爱迪生照明公司总裁爱德华·H. 约翰逊、工厂经理巴切勒先生和我走进了第五大道 65 号对面的一个小地方，那里是爱迪生照明公司的办公室。有人建议大家互相猜一下体重。当我站到秤上时，爱迪生从上到下打量着我，说："特斯拉，重 152 磅[①]，误差一盎司[②]。"爱迪生猜得与秤显示的数据分

---

① 1 磅等于 0.4536 千克。
② 1 盎司等于 28.349 克，16 盎司为 1 磅。

毫不差。当时我穿了厚重的棉衣和鞋子，如果除掉衣物鞋帽，我净重 142 磅，现在我的体重仍然是这个数。我低声对约翰逊先生说："爱迪生怎么可能如此接近地猜出我的体重？""嗯，"他压低了声音说，"我悄悄告诉你，你可千万别告诉别人。爱迪生曾在芝加哥的一家屠宰场工作了很长时间，每天称数千头猪的体重！所以他才猜得这么准。"我信以为真！这很像另外一个情况：我的朋友昌西·M. 迪普给一个英国人讲了一个有关他自己的趣事，这位英国人压根没有听懂，一年之后才回过味儿来，哈哈大笑。我得坦率地承认，我花了比这更长的时间来理解约翰逊讲的笑话。

水中求生

现在看来，我的幸福只是一种谨慎和有节制的生活方式换来的结果。也许最令人想不到的是，在年轻的时候，我曾三度受到重病的摧残，而且医生都认为治愈无望。不仅如此，由于年少无知和放飞自我，我陷入了各种困难、危险和困境之中，依靠一种似魔似幻的力量得到摆脱。我多次溺水，差点儿被活煮，险些被火化，还在被活埋、迷失和冻僵中得以活命。我因疯狗、野猪和其他野生动物多次遇险。我经历了多种可怕的疾病，遇到了各种奇怪的不幸，今天我依然精神矍铄，似乎是一个奇迹。但当我回忆起这些事件时，我确信我能活下来并非全是偶然。

发明家的努力本质上是为了拯救生命，无论他是驾驭力量、改进设备，还是提供新的舒适和便利，他都在增加我们生存的安全性。发明家也比普通人更能在危险中保护自己，因为他观察敏锐且足智多谋。我在一定程度上具有这些品质，就算无法用证据表明，我也会在个人经历中找到它的踪迹。我举一两个例子，请读者自己判断。有一次，大约14岁的时候，我想吓唬一些和我一起洗澡的朋友。我的计划是，在一个长长的漂浮物之下潜水穿越，在另一端突然出现。游泳和潜水对我来说就像鸭子一样自然，我相信我可以完成这项壮举。于是，我一头扎进了水里，转身，在黑暗中迅速朝对面游去。我估计差不多已经安全地越过了这个漂浮物，所以就升到了水面。但令我感到意外的是撞到了漂浮物下面的一根横梁。于是，我迅速潜入水中，快速划水，直到感觉胸中的气体马上就用光了，所以第二次钻出水面，谁想到我的头又碰到了一根横梁，我顿时感到无比紧张。然而，我仍然用尽全力，疯狂地尝试了第三次，结果还是一样。憋气的折磨越来越难以忍受，我的大脑在颤抖，身体在下沉。在那一刻，当我近乎完全绝望时，我感受到了一道亮光，这种亮光有很多，我上方的结构出现在我的视野中。我"看到"或"猜测"水面和横梁上的木板之间有一点空间，依靠一点残存的意识，我浮到水面，嘴巴贴着木板，设法吸了一点空气。不幸的是，空气中夹杂着水沫，把我呛得很厉害。我像在梦中一样重复了几次这个过程，直到我那以可怕的速度跳动的心脏平静下来，我才恢复了镇定。在那之后，我进行了几次不成功的潜水，结果是完全失去了方向感，但是最终逃脱险境。当我冒出水面的时候，小伙伴们已经认为我已溺水而亡，准备打捞我的尸体了。

我的鲁莽毁了那个泳季，但我是好了伤疤忘了疼。仅仅两年后，我就重蹈覆辙，而且比上一次有过之而无不及。当时，在我读书的城市附近有一条河。河上有座大型面粉厂的水坝。通常情况下，水位高出大坝两三英寸①，水在大坝顶部流过。游到那里不是很危险，我经常沉迷其中。一天，我像往常一样独自游到大坝那里玩。

① 1 英寸为 2.54 厘米。

然而，当我离大坝不远时，惊恐地发现水已经上涨并迅速将我冲走。我试图逃离，但为时已晚。幸运的是，我用双手扒住了大坝。我的胸部受到很大的冲击，尽全力使头保持在水面之上。我大声呼救，但周围空无一人，我的声音消失在水流的轰鸣之中。慢慢地，我变得筋疲力尽，再也无法承受了。正当准备放手，任激流把我冲向下面的岩石时，我在一道亮光中看到了一张熟悉的图表。图表中说明了流体的压力与受力面积成正比的基本原理，我自动地向左侧转身。好像施了魔法一样，身体受到的冲击减小了，我发现以这个姿势抵抗水流的力量比较容易。但危险仍然在我面前，我知道自己迟早会被冲下去，因为即使我引起了人们的注意，任何帮助都不可能及时到达我身边。我可以选择主要用我的左手或者右手来扒住大坝，但是我是左撇子，右臂力量相对较小。为此，我不敢换到右边使左手得到休息，只好咬紧牙关，慢慢地推着自己的身体沿着大坝向岸边移动。我身体的左侧贴着大坝，面向面粉厂，背对着岸边，艰难地向后移动。面粉厂那边的水流更急、更深。这是一场漫长而痛苦的磨难，我差一点儿就失败了，因为在移动当中我在大坝上遇到一个坑，差点儿一手抓空。我设法用最后一丝力气脱离了困境。终于到达岸边被别人救起来时，我昏倒了。我的左侧身体被大坝磨得伤痕累累，过了好几个星期才退烧，身体终于恢复。这些只是我诸多遇险中的两个，但它们可能足以表明，如果不是依靠发明家的本能，我早已命丧黄泉了。

钓钩与气枪

对我感兴趣的人经常问我是如何以及何时开始发明的，我只能依靠当前的回忆回答这个问题。我记得第一次尝试是相当雄心勃勃，涉及一种物件的发明和一种方法的发明。物件是早就存在的，但制作方法是我原创的。我的发明之路就此开始了。当时我的一个玩伴得到了一套钓具，这在村里的孩子们之中引起了不小的轰动。第二天早上，小伙伴们都跟着他去钓青蛙。由于和这个男孩吵架，我被排除在行动之外，心中充满了孤独和失望。当时，我从未见过真正的鱼钩，只把它想象成某种奇妙的东西，具有独特的品质。形势所迫，要想去钓青蛙只能自己动手。我找到一段细铁丝，用两块石头将其一端磨尖，再把铁丝弯曲成想象中钩子的形状，并将另一端系在一根结实的绳子上。然后，我砍了一棵小树当钓竿，系上绳子，又找了一些诱饵，来到有很多青蛙的小溪边。我把钩子垂在一只坐在树桩上的青蛙面前，等它上钩。可是，它似乎无动于衷。我几乎要泄气了，但功夫不负有心人。慢慢地，这只青蛙眼睛凸出，身体几乎变为正常大小的两倍，纵身一跃，凶猛地咬住了钩子！

我欣喜若狂立刻把它拉了起来，收入囊中。成功一次，就能成功第二次。我一次又一次地尝试同样的事情，结果证明这个方法是可靠的。那些孤立我的孩子们战果如何呢？他们装备精良，却一无所获。当看到我如此成功时，他们嫉妒得要发疯了。很长一段时间，我保守秘密，享受垄断带来的快乐。最后，我还是本着分享为乐的圣诞精神，把技艺倾囊相授。如此一来，每个男孩都成了钓蛙高手！当然，对青蛙来说，下一个夏天，它们的黑暗时刻真正到来了。

之后，我的发明创造完全是本能驱动——利用自然的能量为人类服务。这次的主角是金龟子，在美国又被称为五月臭虫或六月臭虫，是名副其实的害虫。它们成群结队，数量巨大，乌压压一大片，甚至会压断树枝。该让这些小虫干点活儿了。我做了一个轻杆，将其连在一个大圆盘上，再给圆盘加上轻便的轴，使它可以转动。我捉来四只金龟子，将它们"套"在横杆上，让它们除了向前跑别无选择。这些家伙干活非常卖力，一旦开始，它们就没有停下来的意思，一口气干了几个小时。而且，气温越高，它们的工作就越努力。一切都很顺利，直到来了一个非常奇怪的男孩，他是一名奥地利军队退休军官的儿子。他来到这里，将金龟子生吃活嚼，就像吃美味可口的蓝点牡蛎一样。那令人作呕的景象让人终生难忘，无论让金龟子干活这类事儿多么有前途，我都决定不再继续。从此之后，我再也没有碰过金龟子和其他昆虫。

在那之后，我又迷上了拆装祖父的钟表。我能顺利把钟表大卸八块，却常常无法组装复原。祖父忍无可忍，断然中止了我的折腾。三十年后，我才再一次触碰钟表的发条。不久之后，我开始制造一种由空心管、活塞和两个塞子组成的气枪。开枪时，活塞紧紧抵住身体固定，双手迅速将活塞外面的管子向怀中拉。压缩管中的空气，其压强与温度瞬间升高，接着"呼"的一声，把一只塞子射出去。该技术的核心在于空心管是适当的锥形。我使用那把枪真是得心应手，就是有点儿浪费玻璃。家里窗户上的玻璃都应声而碎，而我也难逃其责。

如果没记错的话，我还喜欢制作剑。剑的原材料很好获取，直接拆家具就行。在塞尔维亚民族诗歌的熏陶下，我对英雄们的壮举充满钦佩。那个时候，我经常手持自制的"利剑"闯入玉米地，对着假想的敌人——玉米秸秆狂砍几个小时。因为破坏了庄稼，母亲狠狠地给了我几记响亮的耳光。这几巴掌不是打给别人看的，而是掷地有声，货真价实。

耻辱与荣耀

以上所说的只是我六岁之前"光荣事迹"的一部分。我出生在斯米连村，并在那里读完了小学一年级。之后，我们搬到了附近的小镇戈斯皮奇。这次搬家对我来说是一场灾难。我舍不得我的鸽子、鸡、羊，还有雄壮威武的鹅群。它们在朝阳的霞光中外出觅食，在落日的余晖里归巢安歇。无论来回，它们都排成整齐的战斗队形，与最优秀的飞行中队相比毫不逊色。与它们的分别让我悲伤心碎。在镇上的新房子里，我只是一个孤独的囚犯，只能透过百叶窗看着来往的路人。我的腼腆令人叹为观止，我宁愿面对一头咆哮的狮子，也不愿面对一个城里的闲汉。我最艰难的考验是周日，我必须打扮

克罗地亚斯米连的尼古拉·特斯拉纪念中心，摄影 Maya Sim Fan。

好去参加礼拜。在那里我遇到了一场意外，一想到这件事，我的血液就立刻凝固成千年的冰川。这是我在教堂的第二次探险。不久前，我曾被困在山上一座人迹罕至的古老小教堂——那里一年只去一次。那是第一次糟糕的经历，但这次更糟。城里有一位富有、善良但自负的女人，经常穿着华丽的衣服来到教堂，拖裙很长，仆人左右相随。一个星期天，我刚敲完钟楼的钟就向楼下冲，而这位贵妇正在楼梯口经过，我一下跃在了她长长的拖裙上。听见"刺啦"一声响，如新兵开枪齐射，又如热油浇入开水——拖裙撕裂了！我父亲气得面红耳赤，扬手就给我一巴掌！那巴掌迅猛地举在空中，却轻轻地落在我的脸颊上。这是父亲对我施过的唯一体罚，我现在仍能记得他的手掌落在脸上的感觉。随之而来的尴尬和难堪无以复加。我处处受到排斥，抬不起头来。直到另一件事情发生，我在别人心目中的形象才有了改观。

一位有进取心的年轻商人组织了一个消防队，购买了一台新的消防车，提供了制服，并对这些人进行了训练，准备进行一场正式演习。这台所谓的消防车涂有漂亮的红色和黑色，带有一台需要 16 名男子操作的水泵。这天下午，正式演习准备就绪，消防车也开到河边。镇上的人们都来见证这前所未有的奇观。当所有的演讲和仪式结束时，抽水的命令下达，机器马达轰鸣。但等了老半天，喷嘴里一滴水也没有流出来。现场的教授和专家试图找出问题所在，但徒劳无功。当失败几乎已成定局时，我到达了现场。虽然我对机器的运行原理一无所知，对气压理论一窍不通，但我到河边本能地摸了摸水中的吸水软管，发现它是瘪的。我断定水下进水口那里有个开关没有打开。于是，我下河摸索着打开了开关，霎时间，一道水柱从喷嘴急射而出，把很多人的漂亮衣服都弄湿了！想当初，阿基米德在叙拉古的街道上赤身裸体地奔跑，并大声喊着"尤里卡"[①]，而我今天的情况也与之差不多。我被人们扛在肩头，前呼后拥，成了大家的英雄。

百步穿杨

在城市安顿下来后，我在所谓的师范学校学习了四年，为我未来的学业做准备。在此期间，我的淘气、努力、成功和麻烦仍在继续。除此之外，我还获得了当地"捕鸦冠军"的独特称号。我的手法简单易行。我在森林里，躲在灌木丛中，模仿鸟儿的叫声，通常我会得到几声鸟儿的回应。不一会儿，一只乌鸦就会扑向我附近的灌木丛。之后就更容易了，我需要做的就是扔一块纸板分散它的注意力，然后在它从灌木丛中飞走之前跳起来抓住它。通过这种方式，我可以捕获尽可能多的乌鸦。但后来发生了一件事，让我开始尊重它们。在和朋友一起回家的路上，我抓到了一对漂亮的乌鸦。当我们离开森林时，成千上万的乌鸦聚集在一起，发出可怕的怒号声。几分钟后，它们发起追击，很快就包围了我

① 希腊语"Eureka"，意为"找到了"。

们。我乐在其中，可是好景不长。后脑勺猛然受到了打击，我一个踉跄摔倒在地。这些乌鸦向我发起猛烈攻击。识时务者为俊杰，我知难而退，被迫释放了这两只乌鸦，跑进山洞与正在那里"避难"的朋友会合。

师范学校的教室里有一些机械模型让我很感兴趣，特别吸引我注意的是水轮机。我建造了许多这样的装置，并反复操作，乐此不疲，简直是一种超级享受。一个事件可以说明我的生活是多么非凡。我叔叔认为我这样做纯属浪费时间，曾不止一次地责备我。我对我读过的尼亚加拉大瀑布的描述很着迷，并在我的想象中描绘了一个由大瀑布提供动力的巨大水轮机。我告诉我叔叔，我会去美国执行这个计划。三十年后，我看到我的想法在尼亚加拉得以实现，对心灵的深不可测的奥秘惊叹不已。

我制作了各种其他的发明和装置，但其中我制作的仿古劲弩是最好的。我射出的箭快似流星，转眼无影无踪，近距离穿透一英寸①厚的松木板毫不费力。通过不断用力拉弓，我的腹肌发达，皮肤变得如鳄鱼皮一样坚硬。我现在甚至能够消化掉小石子，总觉得可能是得益于这项运

① 1英寸等于2.54厘米。

动！我还有一门"飞石击物"的绝技不能不提。凭此绝技，就算到古希腊的竞技场上表演，也会令观众惊叹不已。现在，我将讲述我使用这种古老战争工具的一项壮举，听完之后读者可能会觉得非常难以置信。有一天，我一边练习这门绝技，一边和叔叔在河边散步。那时，夕阳西下，鳟鱼嬉戏，时不时有鱼儿跃出水面。鱼儿在夕阳的照耀下闪闪发光，与它们背后深色的礁石形成鲜明的对比。当然，任何男孩都可能在这些有利条件下击中一条鱼，但我要做的事情比击中一条鱼要困难得多。我向叔叔详细描述了我即将要做的事情："我要打出一块石头，不但要击中鱼儿，还得把它拍到后面的岩石上，断成两半。"我说到做到，一扬手，嗖的一声，鱼儿在岩石上断为两截，与我说得分毫不差！我的叔叔愣愣地看着我，几乎不相信自己的眼睛，随即惊呼道："魔鬼附体了！"过了好几天，我的叔叔才又和我说话，看来把他吓得不轻。我的惊世之举，绝不只这一件，无论多么激动人心，最终也会消失在岁月之中。然而，这些都是我的荣誉，我心安理得享受它们，直到永远。

第三章

旋转的磁场

十岁时，我进入了一所实科中学读书，这是一所新的、设备齐全的机构。在物理系有各种经典科学仪器模型，电气、机械应有尽有。导师们经常进行的演示和实验让我着迷，这无疑是对发明的强大激励！我也热衷于数学研究，并经常因计算速度快而赢得教授的称赞。这是由于我拥有可视化数字运算的能力，不是以通常说的直观方式，而是与现实一样出现在眼前。对复杂的算式，在白板上写出来或是在脑海中出现，对我来说没有任何区别。我无法忍受的是徒手绘图，这占用了大量的时间。其实，我的家庭成员大都在这方面表现出色，不明白为什么我在这方面就不行。我猜想，我讨厌绘图的原因是我只希望用大脑解决问题，做这种绘图训练纯粹是多此一举。如此一来，徒手绘图的成绩就比较差，如果不是有几个特别笨的男孩总是垫底，那么垫底儿的就是我了。这是一个严重的问题，因为在当时的教育体制下，绘画是强制性的，这种缺陷威胁到我的学业。而我父亲在将我从一个班级转到另一个班级时，绘图成绩则给我带来了很大的麻烦。

异想天开

在这个学校的第二年，我开始痴迷于"通过稳定的气压产生连续运动"的想法。我所讲述的消防车事件，点燃了我年轻的想象力，真空的威力也给我留下了深刻的印象。我越来越渴望可以利用这种取之不尽的能量，很长一段时间我都在黑暗中摸索。最后，我的付出最终体现在一项发明中，该发明使我能够实现其他人从未尝试过的事情。

想象一个圆柱体，其两端装上轴承可以自由旋转。这个圆柱体的一部分放在一个截面为矩形的槽中，矩形槽需要与圆柱体贴合得非常好。然后，将槽开口的那一侧封闭。这样，槽中的空间就被圆柱体分成了两部分。为了保证两部分完全隔开，再在两部分的相接处加入一个密闭接头，此接头与圆柱接触但并不影响它转动。密封好之后，两个空间中的一个空间抽成真空，另一个空间则与外界大气相通。至少我这么认为，一个空间有气压，一个空间是真空，圆柱体就会永久转动下去。我按设想建造了一个木制模型并精心安装起来。当我将泵抽掉一个空间的气体，并实际上观察到圆柱体有转动的趋势时，我高兴得发狂——这样我就可以完成我造真空飞行器的梦想了！机械飞行是我想要完成的一件事，但往事不堪回首——我举着雨伞从楼顶上一跃而下，然后重重地摔在地上。之前，我总是梦想能够腾空而起飞向远方，但我不知道怎样才可以做到。现在，上面实验的"成功"让我有了方向。我只需要旋转轴、带翅膀的飞行器，还有一个能提供无限能量的真空器！实现之后，我每天都乘坐舒适和豪华的交通工具进行日常空中旅行，所罗门王的生活也不过如此吧？过了好几年，我才明白大气压对圆柱体表面的作用是多角度的，根本不可能会因我的设计而转动，我观察到的轻微旋转是密封不好漏气所导致的，当两者气压平衡，漏气停止，转动也就停止了。虽然这些知识是逐渐知道的，但还是给了我沉重的打击。这个梦想破灭了。

1894年春天，马克·吐温在尼古拉·特斯拉的实验室里，拿着特斯拉的实验真空灯。该灯由一个线圈供电，该线圈从特斯拉线圈接收电磁能。左侧背景中为特斯拉。

在实科学校刚完成课程后，我就一病不起了。更确切地说，不是一种病，而是几十种疾病。我被认为是病入膏肓，医生们认为我已经无药可医。在此期间，我可以不断地阅读，从一个鲜为人知的公共图书馆借阅图书，并为图书馆对这些图书分类和编目。有一天，我收到了几卷新的文学作品，与我之前读过的书大不相同。这些书让我着迷，以至于让我完全忘记了自己身处重症之中。它们是马克·吐温的早期作品，我觉得正是由于读了这些书，我的病竟然奇迹般地痊愈了。25年后，当我遇到马克·吐温先生并结下深厚友谊时，我将这段经历告诉了他，我惊讶地看到这位幽默大师泪流满面。

人生的选择

我在克罗地亚卡尔施塔特（Carlstadt）的高等实科中学继续学习，我的一位姨妈住在那里。她是一位尊贵的女士，丈夫是久经沙场的上校。在他们家度过的三年令我永生难忘。他家的纪律比战时的军队有过之而无不及，而我，像笼中的金丝雀一样被"精心"喂养。所有的饭菜都质量上乘，美味可口，就是数量少得可怜，只有我饭量的十分之一。我这位姨妈切的火腿薄如纸片。当上校在我的盘子里多放一些食物时，姨妈会立即把它拿走，并煞有介事地说："小心，尼克[1]的饭量很小。"我饭量很大，却只能吃一点点，整日饥肠辘辘，像坦塔罗斯[2]一样受苦。但有一点需要说明，虽然吃不饱，但是我生活在非常精致和艺术气息浓厚的环境中，对于那个时代和条件来讲很不寻常。那里地势低洼，沼泽遍地，虽然我服用了大量的奎宁，但疟疾热一直相伴，从未离

---

[1] 尼古拉·特斯拉的昵称。
[2] 坦塔罗斯是希腊神话中主神宙斯之子，因侮辱众神，被打入地底，饱受折磨。

开。有时河水会上涨，成群的老鼠会涌进家里，吞噬一切，甚至连一捆巨辣的辣椒都完全吃光。但对我来说，抓住这些害人虫却是很好的消遣方式。我通过各种方式围剿它们，这让我在社区中赢得了"老鼠终结者"这个不是太雅的名声。最后，无论怎么说，我的课程完成了，苦难结束了，我获得了成熟的证书，走到了人生的十字路口。

这么多年来，我的父母从未动摇过让我接受神职人员这个职业的决心，光是想到这件事，我就胆战心惊。在我的物理学教授的启发影响下，我对电产生了浓厚的兴趣。他是一个创造性很强的人，经常用他自己发明的仪器来演示电的基本规律。其中，我想起了一个可自由旋转的球状设备，带有锡涂层，如果连上静电发生器，它可以快速旋转。目睹他如此神奇的操作，我激动的心情难以言表。我喜欢这些神秘现象的展示！每一个神奇现象的实现，都会在我的脑海中产生层层波浪。我想更多地了解电这种奇妙的力量，渴望实验和研究。然而，事与愿违，我痛苦万分。

就在我为回家的长途旅行做准备时，我收到了父亲希望我去参加狩猎旅行的消息。这是一个反常的要求，因为他一直极力反对这种运动。但是几天后，我得知了事情的真相，霍乱在家乡肆虐是父亲让我远足的真正原因。但我还是不顾父母的意愿回到了家乡戈斯皮奇。令人难以置信的是，人们对霍乱这个每隔十五年到二十年就袭击该地区一次的祸害是多么的无知。他们认为该病通过空气传播，并带来刺鼻的气味和烟雾。实际上，他们是因为喝了被感染的水，因而成群结队地死去。我在抵达的当天就感染了这种可怕的疾病，尽管九死一生得以生存，但我被困在床上九个月，几乎是一动不动。我觉得自己油尽灯枯，这是第二次发现自己在死亡的门口徘徊。在我弥留之际，我父亲冲进了房间。他脸色苍白，心慌意乱却故作镇定，尽最大所能给我安慰，为我加油打气。我说："也许，如果您让我学习工程学，我还有康复的可能。""你一定能读世界上最好的技术学院！"他郑重地回答，我知道他是认真的。压在我心中的大石头瞬间消失了，我感觉无比的轻松。但如果不是通过一种特殊的豆子的苦汤让我起死回生，我的解脱来得太晚了。我像另一个拉撒路[①]一样满血复活，让大家啧啧称奇。

---

① 拉撒路，圣经里的人物，死后四天被耶稣复活。

奇思妙想

父亲坚持要我花一年时间进行户外体育锻炼以保证健康，我勉强同意了。在这个学期的大部分时间里，我身着猎人装，肩背一捆书，读万卷书，行万里路，遍游名山大川。这种与大自然的接触使我的身体和思想都变得更加强大。我在思考和计划，出现了很多天马行空的想法。对于怎么做，做什么样子，细节犹如在眼前；但这些设想是不是真正符合科学规律，那就不得而知了。例如，在我的一项发明中，提出通过海底管道跨海运送信件和包裹。其具体操作是，把信件和包裹放在球形的可以抗液压的容器中，再把球形的容器放进海底管道，由泵站为管道加压注水，使水流过管道，自然地，载有信件与包裹的容器也就穿过了大海。泵站的输出的水流经过精确计算，其他细节都经过精心设计，只有一个我认为无关紧要的琐碎细节被忽略了。我假设管道中水流的速度不受任何影响，更重要的是，我很高兴将其速度设计得很快。这样，此系统在完美的计算支持下达到了惊人的性能。然而，当思考到管道中的水流受到的阻力之大时，我觉得还是放弃这个发明吧。

我的另一个项目是在围绕地球赤道一周，建造一个可以自由漂浮的环，它随着地球的自转而与地球同步转动，并假定它可以紧急刹车，随时可以不再与地球一起转动。那么，它相对于地球的速度大约是每小时约1000英里[①]。读者会笑，这样的速度在铁路上无异于天方夜谭。我承认，这个计划执行起来很困难——但还没有纽约一位著名教授的计划那么糟糕，他想把空气从炎热地带抽到温带地区，完全忘记了造物主"早有考虑"，已经为此目的提供了一台巨大的"机器"。

还有一个更重要和更有吸引力的计划是从地球的自转中获取能量。由于地球昼夜自转，地球表面的物体也随之移动，若是另有物体沿相反方向移动（或者相对地球不动），两者相遇（相撞或摩擦）会产生巨大的能量。这样就能以最简单的方式利用它来为世界上任何可居住的地区提供动力。当后来我意识到我正处于阿基米德的困境中时，我找不到任何语言来形容我的失望，徒劳地在宇宙中寻找一个支点。

---

① 1 英里约 1.609 千米。

交流电机

假期结束时，我被送到位于施蒂里亚州格拉茨的理工学院，我父亲认为这是一所历史最悠久、声誉最好的学校。那是我热切期待的时刻，在良好的引导下开始了我的学习，并下定决心要取得成功。由于父亲的教导和提供的机会，我以前的培训高于同学们的平均水平。我已经掌握了多种语言的知识，并翻阅了几个图书馆的书籍，获得了或多或少有用的信息。再说一次，我第一次可以随心所欲地选择我的学习方向，再也不用管那些徒手绘画之类的学科了。

我下定决心要给父母一个惊喜，在第一年里，我经常从凌晨三点开始工作，一直工作到晚上十一点，周日和节假日除外。由于我的大多数同学都不爱动脑子，我自然而然地鹤立鸡群。在那一年的课程中，我通过了九门考试，成绩极好，教授们怎么表扬我都不为过。带着他们给我的荣誉，我回家休整，期待着父亲的表扬。然而，我父亲对这些来之不易的荣誉反应冷淡！这让我大失所望，就像泄了气的皮球，这几乎扼杀了我的雄心壮志。但后来，在父亲去世之后，我很痛苦地发现教授给他写的一包信，大意是除非他把我从学校带走，否则我可能会因劳累过度而丧命。

此后，我主要致力于物理、力学和数学研究，闲暇时间在图书馆度过。我是一个名副其实的强迫症患者，即任何事情一旦开始就必须完成！这常常让我进退两难。有一次，我开始阅读伏尔泰的作品。当然，既然开始，也就必须完成。可是令我沮丧的是，这书有将近一百卷，而且都是小字，是那个怪物（指伏尔泰）在每天喝 72 杯黑咖啡时写的。当我把最后一本书读完扔在一边时，我如释重负，并说："再也不会读了！"

我第一年的表现赢得了几位教授的赞赏和友谊，其中包括教授算术和几何的罗格纳教授。珀施尔教授担任理论和实验物理学讲座教授，阿莱博士讲授积分微积分并专门研究微分方程。阿莱博士是我听过的最出色的讲师，他对我的进步特别关心，经常会在教室里待上一两个小时给我答疑解惑，这让我非常高兴。我向他解释了我构思的一种飞行器，它不是一种幻想的发明，而是一种基于严谨的科学原理的飞行器，它已经通过我的涡轮机实现了，并且很快就会被提供给世界。罗格纳教授和珀施尔教授都是很有特点的人。罗格纳有特殊的表达方式，在课堂上，每当他这样做时，在学生中就会发生一阵"骚乱"，然后是长时间而尴尬的停顿。珀施尔教授是一位有条不紊且功底扎实的德国人。他的手脚就像熊掌一样粗壮，但却异常灵巧。他所有的实验都是精准无误、毫无闪失地完成。

在我学习的第二年，我们收到了一台来自巴黎的格拉姆发电机，它具有马蹄形叠层磁场磁铁，以及带有换向器的绕线电枢。它被连接起来，并展示了电流的各种各样的产生方式。当珀施尔教授进行演示时，将机器逆向使用，作为电机运行。但电刷出了问题，火花严重。我注意到这个问题，并认为没有电刷也可以使电机正常工作。然而，珀施尔宣称这是不可能的，并让我就这个主题发表了演讲——对我而言这是一个幸运的事情。在演讲结束时，他说："特斯拉先生要完成一件伟大的事情，但肯定是做不成的。这相当于将保守力（如重力）转化为旋转力。这是一个永动机，一个根本不可能的想法。"但本能是超越知识的东西。毫无疑问，我们拥有某些更精细的直观思维，使我们能够在逻辑推理或大脑的任何其他有意的努力都徒劳无功时，可以感知真理。有一段时间，我因教授的权威而动摇，但很快就相信我是对的，并以青春的热情和无限的信心承担了这项任务。

　　我首先在脑海中想象一台直流电机，运行它并跟踪电枢中电流的变化。然后，我会想象一个交流发电机并研究以类似方式发生的过程。接下来，我将包含电机和发电机的系统可视化，并以各种方式操作它们。我看到的场景对我来说是完全真实和有形的。我在格拉茨的所有剩余时间都是在这种激烈但徒劳无功的努力中度过的，我几乎得出了这个问题无法解决的结论。

攻克旋转磁场难题

　　1880 年，我去了波希米亚的布拉格，按照父亲的愿望，在那里完成了我在大学的学业。正是在那个城市，我取得了决定性的进步，包括将换向器从机器上拆下来，从新的角度研究这个问题，但仍然没有获得想要的结果。在接下来的一年里，我对生活的看法突然发生了变化。我

尼古拉·特斯拉，1879 年

意识到父母为我做出了太大的牺牲，决定减轻他们的负担。美国电话的浪潮刚刚到达欧洲大陆，将在匈牙利的布达佩斯安装电话系统。这似乎是一个理想的机会，更何况我们家人的朋友是企业的负责人。正是在这里，我经历了我所提到的神经的完全崩溃。

我在那段疾病期间所经历的一切都超出了所有人的想象。我的视力和听力总是非凡的。我可以清楚地分辨远处的物体，而别人却连影子也看不到。在童年时代的深夜，我听到微弱的噼啪之声，而其他人都在熟睡。我发出了有火灾的警告，使我们邻居的房子免于火灾。这样的事发生了好几次。

1899 年，我四十多岁，在科罗拉多州进行实验时，可以清楚地听到 550 英里①外的雷声，而我年轻的助手们的听力范围不到 150 英里。因此，我的听觉比普通人敏锐 13 倍以上。然而，与我在神经高度紧张下的敏锐听觉相比，那种听觉的我就是聋子一个。在布达佩斯，我能听到手表的滴答声，而在我和手表之间有三个房间。一只苍蝇落在房间的桌子上，我的耳朵会发出一声闷响。一辆马车从几里外经过，会把我整个人震得摇摇

---

① 1 英里约 1.609 千米。

晃晃。二三十英里外的火车汽笛声使我坐的长凳或椅子振动得如此强烈，以至于疼痛难忍。我脚下的大地不断颤抖。我必须用橡胶垫子支撑我的床才能得到休息。来自远处和近处的大噪声常常产生某种人在说话的效果，如果我不能确认它们究竟是什么声音，我会感到恐惧。如果阳光忽明忽暗，会对我的大脑造成强烈的冲击，可谓是惊心动魄。当我从一座桥或其他结构下面穿过时，头骨承受着巨大的压力，我不得不用我所有的意志力来抵抗。黑暗中，我有一种蝙蝠的感觉，并且可以通过额头上一种奇怪的毛骨悚然的感觉来检测 12 英尺[①] 远的物体。我的脉搏从几下到 260 下不等，身体的所有组织都在抽搐和颤抖，这也许是最难以忍受的。一位著名的医生每天给我服用大剂量的溴化钾，他说我的病极为罕见，无法治愈。

那时我没有经过生理学和心理学专家的诊断，这是我永远的遗憾。我拼命地坚持生活，但从没想过会康复。谁能相信一个如此绝望的残躯会变成一个拥有惊人力量和坚韧的人，能够几乎在没有一天中断情况下工作 38 年——并且发现自己仍然身心健康？我的情况就是这

---

① 1 英尺等于 0.3048 米。

样。生活和继续工作的强烈愿望，以及在一位真诚的运动员朋友的帮助下创造了奇迹。我的健康恢复了，精神也随之恢复了活力。在再次攻克旋转磁场的难题时，我觉得太简单了，还没怎么用力，问题就解决了。当我承担这项任务时，并不是人们通常那样下定决心。对我来说，这是一个神圣的誓言，一个生死攸关的问题。我知道如果我失败了，我就完蛋了。现在我觉得这场战斗已经赢了。在大脑的深处是解决方案，但我还不能表达出来。在我记忆中的一个下午，我和朋友在城市公园散步并朗诵诗歌。在那个年纪，我可以把一整本书一字不差地背诵。其中一本是歌德的《浮士德》。夕阳西下之时，让我想起了那段辉煌的段落：

红日西落，结束一天的劳作

它匆匆而过，探索新的生活

啊，没有翅膀可以把我从泥泞中托起

跟随它翱翔在星光银河

美梦如歌

虽然现在荣耀褪去

哦——举起心灵的翅膀也难掩心中的失落

举起身体的翅膀可以留给我

　　当我说出这些鼓舞人心的话语时，这个想法就像一道闪电一样来了，我如醍醐灌顶，恍然大悟，真理出现在眼前。六年后，我在美国电气工程师协会的演讲中用一根棍子在沙滩上画出了图表，我的同伴完全理解了它们。我看到的图像非常清晰，具有金属和石头的坚固质感，以至于我告诉他："看看我的马达，看我让它反向转动。"我的欣喜难以形容。皮格马利翁看到他的雕像栩栩如生，深受感动，我的感受比他有过之而无不及。一千个我其他的科学发现，也不换我这个发现。这是我不顾一切得来的。

第四章

特斯拉线圈

　　有一段时间，我完全沉浸在对新机器的构想和设计的美好享受之中。这是一种愉悦的精神状态，在我的一生之中熠熠生辉。灵感源源不断地涌来，我唯一的挑战就是牢牢抓住它们。对我来说，我构思的这些装置的每一个细节都是绝对真实和有形的，即使是微小的划痕和磨损都清晰可见。我幸福地想象着各种发动机在飞速转动，在脑海中呈现出一幅让人着迷的景象。当一个人的自然倾向发展成一种强烈的愿望时，他就会以梦为马，朝着目标快速前进。在不到两个月的时间里，我几乎改进了所有类型的电机和系统，并以我的名字命名。也许是天意，为了维持生计，我不得不停止了这种思维创造性活动，去找一份工作。仓促之间，我根据一份电话业务招聘信息来到布达佩斯，无可奈何地接受了匈牙利政府中央电报局的制图员职位。薪水低得可怜，对我来说简直是一种讽刺。幸运的是，我很快就引起了上司的好感，之后我就开始从事与新设备有关的计算、设计和估算工作，直到电话交换机启用。我在工作过程中获得的知识和实践经验是最宝贵的，这份工作给了我充分的机会来发挥我的创造力。我对中央站的设备进行了几项改进，并完善了电话中继器或者说是放大器，它从未获得专利或公开描述，但即使在今天我仍然有发明人的殊荣。为表彰我的高效和贡献，该项目的组织者普斯卡斯先生在处理掉他在布达佩斯的业务后，向我提供了在巴黎的一个职位。当然，我欣然接受了。

巴黎是个神奇的城市，在我脑海中留下了深刻的印象，让我终生难忘。初来乍到的那几天，我在街上四处游逛，觉得什么都新鲜。吸引人的地方很多，让人无法抗拒，只可惜囊中羞涩，工资到手很快就一干二净。当普斯卡斯先生问我的新生活怎么样时，我回答说："其他还好，这月的最后29天最是难熬！"这就是我当时的真实写照。我过着现在被称为"罗斯福式"苦行僧生活。每天早上，无论刮风下雨，我都会从我居住的圣马塞尔大道，到塞纳河上的一个泳池中游泳，跳入水中，游27圈，然后步行一个小时到达公司的工厂所在地艾夫里。七点半，我会在那里吃个伐木工人常吃的早餐，然后急切地盼着午餐时间的到来。同时，我要为爱迪生的亲密朋友和助手、工程经理查尔斯·巴切勒先生剥坚果吃。我台球打得很好，由此和一些美国人成为了朋友。我向他们解释了我的发明，他们中的一位机械部门的工头 D.坎宁安先生提议成立一家股份公司。在我看来，这个提议非常可笑。除了知道这是美国人的做事方式外，我对这意味着什么没有概念。在接下来的几个月里，我不得不从法国和德国之间来回奔波，以解决发电站遇到的麻烦。回到巴黎后，我向公司的一位管理人员劳尔先生提交了一份改进他们发电机的计划，并得到了批准。由于我成功地解决了问题，满意的董事授予我开发自动调节器的特权。不久之后，安装在阿尔萨斯斯特拉斯堡新火车站的照明设备出现了一些麻烦。因为布线有缺陷，在开幕式上，在老皇帝威廉一世出席的情况下，一大块墙壁因短路而被炸毁。德国政府拒绝继续使用此照明设施，法国公司面临严重的损失。由于我对德语的了解和过去的经验，我被赋予了解决问题的艰巨任务，并于

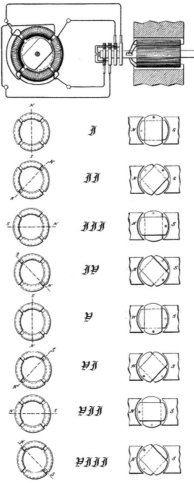

特斯拉 1888 年获得美国专利的交流感应电机的原理图（特斯拉声称在 1882 年设想了这一原理）。

1883 年初动身前往斯特拉斯堡。

那个城市发生的一些事情在我的记忆中留下了不可磨灭的记录。一个奇怪的巧合是，一些在那个时期住在那里的人后来都成了著名的人物！多年后的生活中，我常说："那个老城里有使人变伟大的细菌，其他人都被感染了，唯独没有感染到我！"我在那里的实际工作是与官员们开会或是沟通，这让我日夜劳神。但是，当我有自由时间时，就在火车站对面的一家机械车间建造一个我的简单发电机。对此我早有准备，从巴黎带来了所需要的材料。然而，试验一直推迟到那年夏天才算完成，我终于满意地看到了不同相位的交流电实现的旋转，没有滑动触点或换向器，就像我一年前设想的那样。这是一种美妙的享受，但无法与第一次灵感产生时的喜悦相提并论。

在我的新朋友中，有前任市长博赞先生。我已经在一定程度上让他了解我的这项发明和其他发明，努力争取他的支持。他对我很真诚，把我的项目摆在几个有钱人面前。但令我感到羞愧的是，这些人对此都兴趣索然。博赞先生对我的帮助我铭记于心，1919 年 7 月 1 日我想到了他对我的"另一种帮助"，这种帮助不是对我的经济帮助，而是对我的高度赞赏。1870 年，当德国人入侵时，博赞先生收藏了 1801 年生产的圣埃斯蒂菲酒。他认为，只有我才配得上喝这种酒。可以说，这是我所提到的令人难忘的事件之一。他敦促我尽快返回巴黎并在那里寻求资金支持——这正是我迫切需要的。然而，由于我遇到了各种各样的小麻烦，我的工作和洽谈一再拖延，有时让我感觉前途一片暗淡。

为了说明德国人的"严谨"和"效率"，我在这里提到一个相当有趣的经历。一盏 16 烛光[①] 的白炽灯将被放置在走廊上，在选择了合适的位置后，我命令机械师布线。忙活了一段时间后，他得出了结论：必须咨询工程师，然后他就这么做了。工程师提出了一些不同意见，但最后同意将灯放置在距离我指定的位置 2 英寸[②]的地方，于是工作继续。不久，工程师似乎心里越来越没底，告诉我应该通知检查员阿弗戴克——一个重量级的人物。在调查、辩论之后，阿弗戴克决定将灯向后移动 2 英寸——这是我原来标记的地方。然而，没过多久，阿弗戴克自己就冷静下来，并告诉我他已将此事通知高级督察希罗尼穆斯，应该等待他的决定。过了几天，高

---

① Candlepower，c.p.，发光强度单位。一个烛光单位约为 0.981 坎德拉。
② 2 英寸等于 5.08 厘米。

级督察才能够从其他繁忙的公务中解脱出来。虽然有所延误，但他毕竟到了。进行了两个小时的辩论，高级督察决定将灯再移开2英寸。我想，这次应该是最后的折腾了吧？然而，我错了。弄了半天这位高级督察也决定不了，他对我说："冯克议员非常讲究，我不敢在没有他明确同意的情况下下令把这盏灯放置在此处。"那就让这位大议员来看看吧。我们一大早就开始扫地、擦玻璃，窗明几净一尘不染。每个人都起立迎接，为表示尊敬我还戴上了手套！当冯克带着他的随从来到时，受到了隆重的接待。他考虑了两个小时，突然喊道："我得走了！"要离开时，他指着天花板上的一个地方，命令我把灯放在那里——这就是我最初确定的位置。

日子一天天过去，但我决心不惜一切代价实现目标，最终我的努力得到了回报。到1884年春天，所有的问题都得到了解决，工厂正式验收通过，问题得到解决，我满怀期待地回到了巴黎。一位经理向我承诺，如果我成功了，将给予我丰厚的补偿，并公平地考虑我在他们的发电机上所做的改进，我盼着能得到一大笔钱。为方便起见，我将三个经理指定为A、B和C。当我打电话给A时，他告诉我B有发言权。B认为只有C可以决定，而 C 非常确定只有 A 才有权力采取行动。经过几圈这样的循环后，我突然意识到我的奖励是空中楼阁，可能永远也无法兑现。我试图为发展筹集资金的尝试，也以失败告终。我对这个地方失望透顶。当巴切勒先生劝我去美国重新设计爱迪生机器时，我决定去黄金应许之地试试运气。结果，差点就去不成了。我变卖了那点微不足道的家当，换得川资路费。到了火车站，当火车马上就要出发时，那一刻，我发现身上的钱和车票都不翼而飞了！怎么办？大力士赫拉克勒斯有足够的时间来考虑，但我只能眼睁睁看着火车飞驰而去。我的大脑突突跳得厉害，就像振荡电路一样。我努力使自己平静下来，在关键时刻做出了正确的判断。我要乘船到美国。经历告诉我，无论心情是好还是坏，正确的选择和要做的事情不会变。我带上所剩无几的东西：一些我写的诗和文章，以及一个与不可解积分的解和我的飞行器有关的计算材料。在航行中，我大部分时间都坐在船尾，等待有人失足落水之时去救援，丝毫没有想到自己的危险。后来，当我吸收了一些务实的美国观念时，我不禁后怕不已，并惊叹于我以前的愚蠢。

与爱迪生的合作

　　我希望我能用语言表达我对这个国家的第一印象。在《阿拉伯故事》中，我读到了精灵如何将人们运送到梦幻之地，过着愉快的冒险生活。我的情况正好相反。精灵把我从一个梦幻的世界带入了一个现实世界。我过

爱迪生员工查尔斯·克拉克拍摄的 1881 年爱迪生机械厂（前身为埃特纳钢铁厂）的照片，位于曼哈顿。爱迪生机械厂是一家制造公司，旨在生产发电机、大型电动机以及 19 世纪 80 年代由爱迪生在纽约市建造的电气照明系统的其他组件。特斯拉发现，从国际化的欧洲到这样一个"落后"的地方工作，有些不适应。

往的一切都是美丽、艺术和迷人的；我在这里看到的是机械和粗糙，毫无吸引力。一个身材魁梧的警察正在转动他的手杖，在我看来这手杖就像一根大木棒。我礼貌地走近他问路。"往下六个街区，然后左转！"他说，眼中带着冷酷。"这是美国吗？"我痛苦而不解地问自己，"它在文明方面落后于欧洲一个世纪。"当我在 1889 年出国时——我到这里已经五年——我开始相信，欧洲的确领先了一百多年，直到今天还没有任何事情能改变我的看法。

与爱迪生的会面是我一生中难忘的事件。我对这位了不起的人感到吃惊。爱迪生没有早期的优势和科学训练，却取得了如此多的成就。我学过十几种语言，钻研文学和艺术，并在图书馆度过了一生最美好的岁月，阅读了各种各样的书，从牛顿的《原理》到保罗·德科克的小说。当时，我觉得我的大部分生命都被浪费了。但没过多久，我就意识到这是我能做得最好的事情。几周之内，我就赢得了爱迪生的信任，事情就是这样发生的。

当时最快的客运轮船"SS 俄勒冈州"号的两台照明设备都无法使用，航行被推迟。由于船的上层建筑是在电力设备安装后建造的，因此无法将它们从舱中移除。情况很严重，爱迪生非常恼火。晚上，我带着必要的仪器登上了这艘船，准备干通宵。发电机状况不佳，有几次短路和断路，但在机组人员的帮助下，我成功地将它们恢复至良好状态。早上五点，在去商店的路上经过第五大道时，我遇到了爱迪生和巴切勒以及其他几个人，他们正准备回家休息。"这是我们的巴黎人在晚上跑来跑去，"他说。当我告诉他我来自"俄勒冈州"号并且已经修理了两台机器时，他沉默地看着我，然后一言不发地走开了。但当他走了一段距离后，我听到他说："巴切勒，这是一个非常好的人！"从那时起，我就可以完全自由地指导这项工作了。在将近一年的时间里，我的正常工作时间是从上午10点半到第二天早上5点，没有一天例外。爱迪生对我说："我有很多勤奋的助手，但你是最勤奋的。"在此期间，我设计了24种不同类型的短芯、统一图案的标准机器，以取代旧机器。经理答应我完成这项任务奖励我五万美元，但结果是一个恶作剧。这给了我一个痛苦的打击，我辞职了。

特斯拉线圈的产生

紧接着，有人向我提出以我的名义成立弧光灯公司的建议，我同意了①。我认为，终于有机会大展宏图制造交流发电机了。但当我向我的新同事提出这个话题时，他们说："不，我们想要弧光灯。我们不在乎你的这个交流发电机。"1886 年，我的电弧照明系统得到完善，并被用于工厂和市政照明。但实际上我被抛弃了，除了精美雕刻的空头股票证书外，一无所有。然后在我不适合的新领域进行了一段时间的难熬工作，但最终得到了回报。1887 年 4 月，特斯拉电气公司成立②，提供了实验室和设施。我在那里制造的电机，与我想象的完全一样。我没有尝试改进设计，只是把我的视觉和视觉上出现的图片复制到现实之中，丝毫不差。

1888 年年初，特斯拉电气公司与西屋公司达成一项大规模生产电动机的协议，但仍有很大的困难需要克

① 离开爱迪生公司后不久，特斯拉开始申请弧光照明系统的专利，1885年 3 月，他会见了专利律师莱缪尔·W. 瑟雷尔，以获得提交专利的帮助。瑟雷尔将特斯拉介绍给了两位商人罗伯特·莱恩和本杰明·韦尔，他们同意以特斯拉的名义资助一家弧光灯制造和公用事业公司。特斯拉在这一年剩余时间里的工作，获得了包括改进的直流发电机在内的专利，这是特斯拉在美国获得的第一批专利。

② 1886 年年底，特斯拉遇到了西联主管阿尔弗雷德·S. 布朗和纽约律师查尔斯·弗莱彻·佩克，此二人在设立公司和专利转化方面经验丰富。他们认同特斯拉的想法并同意给予资金支持，并于 1887 年 4 月共同成立了特斯拉电气公司，并达成协议，产生的专利利润将 1/3 归特斯拉，1/3 归佩克和布朗，1/3 为发展提供资金。公司在曼哈顿自由街 89 号为特斯拉建立了一个实验室，在那里特斯拉致力于改进和开发新型电动机、发电机和其他设备。

服。我的系统是基于低频电流的使用，西屋专家采用了每秒 133 个周期（即频率为 133 赫兹）的电流，以确保在改造中的优势。他们不想偏离他们的标准设备形式，我必须集中精力使电机适应这些条件。另一个必要条件是生产一种能够在两根电线上以这种频率有效运行的电机，这并不容易实现。

然而，在 1889 年年底，我已完成匹兹堡的任务 ①，回到纽约并在格兰街 ② 的一个实验室继续实验工作。在那里我立即开始了高频发电机（特斯拉线圈）③的研发设计。这是一个崭新而新奇的领域，之前从未有人涉足，因此很多困难接踵而来。我放弃了感应发电机的方案，因为担心它可能不会产生完美的正弦波，而这对谐振动

---

① 西屋公司在匹兹堡，特斯拉应邀到匹兹堡解决西屋公司的技术难题。
② 特斯拉从他的交流电专利许可中赚到的钱使他经济独立，并使他有时间和资金追求自己感兴趣的事物。1889 年，特斯拉搬出佩克和布朗租用的自由街住所，搬入格兰街 175 号的实验室（1889—1892）。在接下来的十几年中，他在曼哈顿的一系列车间或实验室中工作。南第五大道 33—35 号的四楼（1892—1895）以及东豪斯顿街 46 号和 48 号的六楼和七楼（1895—1902）。特斯拉和他雇用的工作人员在这些车间里进行他最重要的一些工作。
③ 指 1889 年夏天，特斯拉前往 1889 年巴黎世界博览会，了解到海因里希·赫兹在 1886—1888 年的实验证明了包括无线电波在内的电磁辐射的存在。特斯拉发现这一新发现"令人耳目一新"，并决定对其进行更全面的探索。特斯拉尝试用他一直在开发的高速交流发电机为线圈供电，提出了他的"振荡变压器"，用于产生高压、小电流、高频的交流电，后来被称为特斯拉线圈。

作非常重要。如果不是这个原因，我就可以为自己节省大量的精力。高频交流发电机的另一个令人沮丧的缺点，就是速度的不稳定，这可能会严重限制其使用。我在向美国电气工程师学会演示时已经注意到，有好几次调谐失灵了，得重新调整。很久之后我找了解决问题的方法，只要在载荷范围内，其速度就基本恒定，每个周期速度的变化微不足道。

从许多其他方面综合考虑，似乎发明一种更简单的装置来产生振荡电流更好。1856 年，开尔文勋爵揭示了电容放电的理论，但没有对这一重要知识进行实际应用。我看到了可能性，并根据这个原理进行了感应发电机的开发。我的研发非常神速，以至于我在1891 年的演讲中展示了一个线圈发出了 5 英寸[①] 火花。那次我坦率地告诉工程师，新方法在电力传送时存在一个缺陷，即火花间隙的损失。随后的研究表明，无论使用什么介质，无论是空气、氢气、汞蒸气、油还是电子流，效率都是一样的。这非常类似于控制机械能转换的定律。我们可以从某个高度垂直放下一个重物，或者沿着任何迂回的路径将它带到较低的位置，

---

① 5 英寸等于 12.7 厘米。

尼古拉·特斯拉于 1891 年在纽约哥伦比亚大学演示电力和高频能量的无线传输。这两个金属片连接到他的特斯拉线圈振荡器，该振荡器施加了一个以射频振荡的高压。电场使他拿着的长的、部分抽空的盖斯勒管中的气体电离（类似于现代霓虹灯），使它们在没有电线的情况下发光。

对重力做功来说没有区别。然而幸运的是，这个缺点并不是致命的，因为通过适当比例的谐振电路，可以达到 85% 的效率。从我宣布特斯拉线圈的发明到今天，它已被普遍使用，并在许多部门引发了一场革命。但更伟大的未来在等待着它。1900 年，当我获得 100 英尺[①]的强大放电并引起全球轰动时，我想起了我在格兰街实验室观察到的第一个微小火花，这与我发现旋转磁场时的感觉类似，都让我激动不已。

————————————

① 约 30.48 米。

第五章

放大发射器

当我回顾我以前的事件时，我意识到事情对我们命运的影响是多么微妙。我年轻时经历的一个事件可以说明。某个冬日，我和其他男孩一起爬上了一座陡峭的山。积雪很深，但温暖的南风却很适宜。我们玩滚雪球的游戏，将一个雪球从山坡上掷下，雪球落下会沾上积雪向山下滚动，沾的积雪越多，雪球就越大，滚得就越远。我们试图在这项激动人心的运动中超越对方。突然看到一个雪球越滚越大，越滚越快，超出了我们的想象，膨胀到了巨大的比例，直到它变得像房子一样大，并以一种让地面颤抖的力量轰然坠入下方的山谷。我目瞪口呆，无法理解发生了什么。几个星期后，我看到了雪崩的照片。我想知道一个小小的雪球，是怎样长到一个巨型雪球的。从那时起，我就着迷于微弱作用的放大。多年后，当我开始从事机械和电气共振的实验研究时，我从一开始就对它产生了浓厚的兴趣。可能如果不是因为那个大雪球给我留下了深刻的印象，我可能不会进一步研究我用线圈获得的小火花，并且永远不会开发出我最好的发明，我将在这里第一次讲述这段真实的历史。

涡轮机

一些好事者经常问我，我最看重自己的哪些发现。这取决于视角。不少技术人员，在他们的特殊部门非常有能力，但思想迂腐、目光短浅。他们声称除了感应电动机之外，我几乎没有给世界带来任何实际用途。这真是大错特错！一个新的想法不能以它的直接结果来判断。作为对紧迫工业问题的长期寻求答案的结果，我的交流输电系统应运而生。尽管必须克服相当大的阻力并调和对立的利益，但像往常一样，商业推广拖延太久。这种情况与我的涡轮机发明后面临的情况差不多。人们应该认为，如此简单而美丽的发明，具有理想电动机的许多特征，应该立即投入使用。这次发明与之前的情况比较类似，都是一波三折，但旋转磁场还是有它的特别之处。旋转场的预期效果并不是使现有的机器变得毫无价值，相反它是为了赋予现有的机器额外的价值。该系统既适用于新企业，也适用于旧企业的改进。我的无叶涡轮机则是一项革命性的发明。从某种意义上说，它的成功意味着放弃已经花费数十亿美元的陈旧类型的原机器，这是一个根本性的背离。在这种情况下，进展必须缓慢，也许最大的障碍是有组织的反对派在专家头脑中形成的偏见。

就在前几天，我遇到了我的朋友和前助理查尔斯·F. 斯科特，他已经成了耶鲁大学电气工程教授。这次见面是一个令人沮丧的经历。我已经很久没有见到他了，很高兴有机会在我的办公室里聊聊天。我们的谈话自然而然地转移到我的涡轮机上，这让我兴奋得过了头。"斯科

查尔斯·F. 斯科特

特，"我惊呼道，被美好未来的愿景迷住了，"我的涡轮机将淘汰世界上所有的热力发动机。"斯科特摸了摸下巴，若有所思地移开视线，仿佛在做心算。"你的涡轮机就是一堆垃圾！"说完之后，他就一声不吭地离开了！

其实，我的这些发明只不过是朝着某些方向改进。在改进它们时，我只是按照与生俱来的感觉来改进现有的设备，而没有特别考虑服务于我们更为迫切的需求。"放大发射器"是我多年奋斗的结果，其主要目标是解

1899 年前后，尼古拉·特斯拉与他的放大发射器在科罗拉多斯普林斯的实验室（合成照片）。这张照片是摄影师狄肯森·V.艾利的宣传噱头，采用双重曝光。首先在黑暗的房间里拍摄机器巨大的火花，然后在关闭机器和特斯拉坐在椅子上的情况下再次曝光照相底片。

决对人类来说非常重要的问题，远比单纯的工业发展更有意义。

如果我没记错的话，那是在 1890 年 11 月，我进行了一项实验，这是科学史上非凡和壮观的实验之一。在研究高频电流的特征时，我对自己感到满意的是，可以用足够强度的电场来点亮无电极真空管。因此，我建造了一个变压器来测试该理论，首次试验证明了巨大的成功。很难理解那些奇怪的现象在当时意味着什么。人们渴望新鲜的感觉，但很快就会对它们漠不关心。昨天的奇迹是今天的习以为常。当我的管子第一次公开展出时，它们的表现令人惊叹，无法形容。我收到了来自世界各地的紧急邀请，向我提供了无数荣誉和其他讨人喜欢的诱惑，但是我拒绝了。

然而，在 1892 年，这些要求变得不可抗拒。我去了伦敦，在那里我在电气工程师学会发表了演讲。我本来打算按照类似的要求立即启程前往巴黎，但詹姆斯·杜瓦爵士坚持让我出席皇家学会。我是一个有坚定决心的人，但很容易屈服于这位伟大的苏格兰人的有力论据。他把我推到椅子上，倒了半杯美妙的棕色液体，闪烁着各种彩虹色，尝起来像花蜜。"现在，"他说，"你坐在法拉第的椅子上，享受着他曾经喝过的威士忌。"在这两个方面，这都是令人羡慕的经历。第二天晚上，我在该机构进行了演讲，在演示结束时，雷利勋爵向听众发表了讲话，他慷慨的话语给我带来了动力。人们对我的追捧让我难以消受，我逃离伦敦，又逃离巴黎，然后回到我的家，在那里我经历了最痛苦的磨难和疾病。恢复健康后，我开始制定赴美复工计划。在那之前，我从未意识到我拥有发明家的任何特殊的天赋，但我一直认为是理想的科学家的雷利勋爵都这么说了，我也就当真了，我觉得我应该专注于一些大的研究项目。

闪电的启示

一天，当我在山中漫游时，乌云滚滚，感觉暴风雨顷刻之间就会来到。天空变得越来越黑暗，但雨不知道在等待什么，还是不肯降落。突然，一道闪电划破长空，一声惊雷滚过，紧接着大雨倾盆。这个观察让我思考。很明显，闪电与降雨，这两种现象是密切的因果关系。稍微思考一下，我就得出结论，雨在降落的时候，电能是微不足道的。划过长空的闪电，很像一个敏感的扳机触发了大雨。

如果闪电是降雨的开关，这就有促成一个伟大的发明的可能性。如果我们能获得驾驭闪电的能力，那么整个星球以及它的生存条件都可以由此改变。太阳升华起海洋中的水，风把它吹到遥远的地方，在那里它保持着最微妙的平衡状态，等待着自然闪电的触发。如果我们有能力在人类需要的时间和地点破坏它，那么我们就可以随意控制维持地球上能影响生命的水系。我们可以灌溉干旱的沙漠，创造湖泊和河流，提供无限量的动力。这将是利用太阳为人类所用的最有效方式。但问题是：我们可以驾驭闪电吗？或者有能力制造出闪电吗？这似乎是痴人说梦，但我下定决心一试。1892 年夏天，当我回到美国后，立即开始了如何实现电力的无线传输这项对我来说更有吸引力的工作。

第一个令人满意的结果出现在第二年的春天，我的锥形线圈达到了大约 100 万伏的电压。就现在的技术而言，这不算什么，但当时它被认为是一项壮举。直到 1895 年我的实验室被大火烧毁为止，这个项目一直取得稳步进展，这可以从 T. C. 马丁发表在《世纪》杂志 4 月号上的一篇文章来判断。这场大火让我在很多方面都退步了，那一年的大部分时间都必须致力于规划和重

1896年，特斯拉在他位于纽约东休斯顿街的实验室里，在他的高压特斯拉线圈变压器的螺旋线圈前，拿着鲁杰·博斯科维奇的著作《自然哲学理论》。

建。然而，只要情况允许，我就会回到原来的任务中。

虽然我知道使用更大尺寸的设备可以获得更高的电压，但我本能地认为可以通过适当设计一个相对较小和紧凑的变压器来实现该目标。如我的专利所示，在对扁平螺旋形式的次级线圈进行测试时，没有电流产生，这让我感到惊讶。不久之后我发现这是由于所绕线圈的位置及其相互作用出现了问题。从这一观察中获益，我采用了粗一些的电线绕成线圈，而且每匝之间有适当的距离，以抑制分布电容，同时防止电荷在任何点的过度积累。这一原理的应用使我能够产生 400 万伏的电压，这大约是我在休斯顿街的新实验室所能达到的极限，因为放电延伸了 16 英尺[①]的距离。这张发射机发射电弧的照片发表在 1898 年 11 月的《电气评论》上。

为了进一步研究此项目，我不得不进行露天实验。1899 年春天，在完成了建立无线工厂的准备工作后，我去了科罗拉多州，在那里待了一年多。在这里，我完成了其他改进，可以产生任何可能需要的电压电流。有兴趣的人会在我 1900 年 6 月于《世纪》杂志上发表的文章"增加人类能量的问题"中找到一些关于我在那里进

① 约 4.88 米。

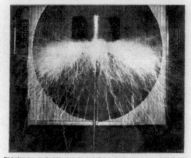

1898 年 11 月的《电气评论》刊登的特斯拉发射机的照片及文章。

行实验信息,我在之前的场合曾提到过。

《电气实验员》杂志要求我在这个问题上说得很清楚,以便杂志读者中我的青年朋友们清楚地了解我的"放大发射器"的构造和操作以及它的用途。首先,它是一个带有次级的谐振变压器,其中充电到高电位的部

特斯拉在科罗拉多州科罗拉多斯普林斯的高压实验室，他在1899年至1900年进行了无线电力传输实验。伸缩塔顶部的铜球，是他巨大的放大发射器的终端。本质上是一个巨大的特斯拉线圈，它可以在150千赫兹的频率下产生大约2000万伏的射频电势，产生数百英尺[①]长的巨大电弧。

件具有相当大的面积并使电荷沿着理想的空间排列。包络表面具有非常大的曲率半径，并且彼此之间保持适当的距离，从而确保各处的电荷表面密度很小，因此即使导体裸露也不会发生泄漏。它适用于任何频率，从每秒几个循环到几千个循环，可用于产生大电流和中等电压，或小电流和大电压。最大电压仅取决于带电元件所在表面的曲率和后者的面积。

---

① 100英尺等于30.48米。

从我的经验来看，产生高达 1 亿伏的电压是完全可行的。另一方面，可以在天线中获得数千安培的电流。这种性能需要一个尺寸合适的场所。从理论上讲，直径小于 90 英尺[①]的线圈足以产生该量级的电压，而对于通常频率下，2000—4000 安培的天线电流，其直径不需要大于 30 英尺[②]。

在更严格的意义上，特斯拉线圈是这样一种发射器，其中赫兹波辐射与整个能量相比是一个完全可以忽略的量，在这种情况下，阻尼因子非常小，并且在提升的容量中存储了巨大的电荷。这样的电路可能会被任何类型的脉冲激励，即使是低频脉冲，它也会像交流发电机一样产生正弦和连续的振荡。

然而，从该术语的最狭义来看，它是一种谐振变压器，除了具有这些品质外，它还具有精确的比例以适合地球及其电气常数和特性，凭借这种设计，它实现了能量的无线传输，然后绝对消除了距离对脉冲强度的影响。根据精确的数学定律，甚至可以使脉冲随着与目标的距离增大而增加。

---

① 约 27.4 米。
② 约 9.1 米。

这项发明是我的"世界系统"中包含的众多发明之一。我在 1900 年回到纽约时承诺将无线传输商业化。至于我的企业的直接目的，在我引用的那个时期的技术声明中明确概述了它们：

"世界体系"是发明者在长期持续的研究和实验过程中的几个原始发现的结合。它不仅使任何类型的信号、消息或字符能够即时、精确地无线传输到世界各地，而且使现有的电报、电话和其他信号站的互联成为可能，而不会对原设备做大的改变。例如，利用现有的设备，电话用户可以呼叫地球上的任何其他用户并与之畅谈。一个小巧且便宜的接收器，将使他能够在陆地或海上的任何地方聆听演讲或在其他地方播放的音乐，无论距离多远。引用这些例子只是为了说明这一伟大科学进步的可能性，它消除了距离，使完美的自然导体——地球，可用于人类的各种需求。这样做的一个影响深远的结果是，任何能够通过一根或多根电线（明显受限的距离）操作的设备，同样可以在没有人工导体的情况下以相同的设施和精度被驱动，仅受地球的物理尺寸所限。因此，这种理想的传输方式不仅会为商业开发开辟全新的领域，而且旧的领域也会有相当大的扩展。

"世界系统"基于以下主要发明和发现的应用：

1. 特斯拉线圈。该设备用于产生电振荡，就像火药在战争中一样具有革命性。发明者用这种仪器已经产生了比以往任何时候都强许多倍的电流，并且产生了超过100英尺①长的火花。

2. 放大发射器。这是特斯拉最好的发明，一种特殊的变压器，专门用于激发地球，它在传输电能方面就像望远镜在天文观测中一样。通过使用这个奇妙的装置，已经建立了比闪电更大强度的电流，足以点亮两百多个白炽灯。

3. 特斯拉无线系统。该系统包括许多改进，并且是已知的唯一一种无需电线即可将电能经济地传输到远处的方法。对发明者在科罗拉多州建立的一个活跃的实验站进行的仔细测试和测量表明，可以传输任何所需数量的电力，如有必要，可以在全球范围内传输，损失不超过百分之几。

4. 信息加密传递。特斯拉的这项发明是对原始信息的"调整加工"，就像对精确的语言进行加密表达一样。它使信号或消息的传输成为可能，无论是在主动发送方面还是被动接受方面，都具有绝对保密和排他性，即不

① 约30.48米。

干扰和不可干扰。每个信号就像一个具有明确身份的个体，几乎没有对站点或仪器的数量限制，可以同时操作而不会受到最轻微的相互干扰。

5. 陆地静止波。人们普遍解释说，这一奇妙的发现意味着地球对特定音高的电振荡做出反应，就像对某些声波的音叉一样。这些特殊的电气振荡，能够强烈地激发地球，使其在商业和许多其他方面具有非常重要的无数用途。

第一个"世界系统"发电厂可在九个月内投入运行。有了这个发电厂，实现高达1000万马力的电力输送将是切实可行的。该系统旨在为尽可能多的技术成果提供服务，而非是为了盈利。其中可以提到以下几点：

（1）全球现有电报局的互联互通；

（2）建立秘密的、不可干扰的政府电报服务；

（3）全球所有现有电话交换机或办公室的互联；

（4）通过电报或电话，一般新闻的普遍发行；

（5）建立这样一个专供私人使用的情报传输"世界体系"；

（6）全球所有股票代码的互联互通和运行；

（7）建立音乐发行等"世界体系"；

（8）廉价的时钟以天文的精确方式显示时间，无须任何关注；

（9）打字或手写字符、字母、支票等的世界传输；

（10）建立海洋通用服务体系，使所有船舶的导航员无需指南针即可完美操舵，确定准确位置、时间和航速，防止碰撞和灾难等；

（11）世界陆地和海上印刷系统的启动；

（12）世界范围内复制摄影图片和各种图纸或记录。

我还提议在无线传输电力方面进行小规模但足以让人信服的示范。除了这些，我还提到了我的发现的其他更重要的应用，这些应用将在未来的某个日期公开。

长岛建有一座工厂，塔高 187 英尺①，球形终端直径约 68 英尺②。这些尺寸足以传输几乎任何大小的能量。最初只传输 200 — 300 千瓦，但我打算以后要到几千马力③。发射器要发射一种特殊的波复合体，我设计了一种独特的电话控制方法，可以控制任何数量的能量。

这座塔在两年前被拆除，但我的项目仍在开发中，另一个在某些功能上有所改进的项目将被建造。在这种情况下，我要反驳广为流传的报道，即由于战争之故，

① 约 57 米。

② 约 20.7 米。

③ 1 马力 =0.736 千瓦。

尼古拉·特斯拉的沃登克里夫发射塔，位于纽约州肖勒姆，摄于 1904 年。该实验设施由特斯拉于 1901 年至 1904 年在华尔街银行家摩根的支持下建造，旨在成为跨大西洋无线电报站和无线电力发射器，但从未完工。该塔于 1916 年被拆除。

政府拆除了该建筑。这可能会使有些人对我抱有偏见，他们可能不知道我的保险箱中一直有三十年前授予我美国荣誉公民的证书。我的勋章、文凭、学位、金牌和其他荣誉都装在旧箱子里。如果上面的谣言确有其事，那倒是个好事，政府得给我一大笔钱赔偿我建塔的损失。实际上，保护这塔才符合政府的利益，因为它本来可以——仅提及一个有价值的结果——在它的帮助下可以定位任何位置的潜艇。我的工厂、服务和我所有的改进一直由官员支配。自从欧洲冲突爆发以来，我一直在贡献空中导航、船舶推进和无线传输有关的发明，因为这对国家来说是最重要的。那些消息灵通的人都知道，我的想法已经彻底改变了美国的工业。我不知道有哪一个发明家在这方面和我一样幸运，特别是在战争中用到的改进或发明。我以前没有就这个话题公开表达过自己的看法，因为在全世界都陷入严重困境的时候，反而陈述自己的贡献似乎是不太妥当。

鉴于针对我的各种谣言，我还要补充一点，J. 皮尔庞特·摩根先生对我的兴趣并不是在商业方面，而是出于他帮助许多其他先驱者的同样的伟大精神。他慷慨兑现了他的承诺，不应当再有别的奢求。他对我的成就给予了最高的评价，并以实际行动证明他完全相信我有能力最终实现我的目标。我不愿意让一些心胸狭窄和嫉妒我的人因挫败了我的努力而感到洋洋自得，这些人对我来说只不过是一种令人讨厌的致病的微生物。我的计划是因自然规律而受阻，世界并没有为此做好准备——它太超前了。然而，自然规则是不变的，历史车轮滚滚向前，先进的技术一定会取得胜利。

第六章

远程控制及传送技术

我所涉足的任何学科中，最需要集中精力而为的就是将放大发射器作为基础的系统，为此我可谓是绞尽脑汁，殚精竭虑。之前，我把自己青春的热情和活力都投入到旋转磁场发现的开发中，那时的工作性质与现在完全不同。即便也是耗时费力，但不像现在这样，解决这些诸如无线传送能量之类百思不得其解的问题。这些问题让我用尽了所有敏锐的洞察力。当时的我体能甚佳，但也在即将看到胜利曙光时精力耗尽，整个人完全崩溃了。

生命的保护机制

毫无疑问，这种崩溃其实是一种自我保护机制，撑不住了就自动病倒。如果不是老天爷为我配备了这种神奇的机制，我以后会付出更大的代价——我的职业生涯很可能会提前终止。只要这种机制运行，我就不会因为过度工作而一命呜呼。又因为我完全不像其他人一样需要有休息和假期，如果从不病倒，那别的发明家也就没啥事可做了。当我筋疲力尽时，我就会像黑人一样倒头就睡，而不像白人那样瞻前顾后难以入眠。如果非要探索一个理论，我想我的身体可能会逐渐积累一定数量的某种有毒物质，使我陷入几乎昏昏欲睡的状态。这种状态会持续半小时，一分钟不多。醒来后，我有一种感觉，好像刚刚发生的事情已经是很久以前，如果我试图继续原来的思路，我会感到精神性的恶心，根本无法进行。然后我不由自主地转向困难的工作，惊讶地发现之前无法解决的问题能迎刃而解。同样，数周或数月后，我对原本暂时放弃的发明的灵感和热情又回来了，总是不费吹灰之力就能找到所有难题的答案。

在这方面，我将讲述一个心理学专业学生可能会感兴趣的非凡经历。我用接地的发射器产生了惊人的现象，并正在努力确定它与通过土壤传播电流的关联。这似乎是一项无望的工作，一年多来，我坚持不懈，但徒劳无功。我完全专注于这项研究，以至于我忘记了一切，甚至忘记了我是带病工作。最后，当我快要崩溃的时候，我的保护机制被触发了，身体分泌的"保护剂"让我陷入到沉睡之中。恢复清醒之后，我惊愕地意识到，除了婴儿时期的事情不记得，其他的场景一幕幕出现在眼前。神奇的是，这些场景以惊人的清晰度出现在我的视野中，让我感到欣慰。夜复一夜，每天晚上入睡的时候，我都会想起它们，之前的记忆也越来越多地出现在脑海。我母亲的形象始终是慢慢展开的景象中的主要人物，再次见到她的强烈渴望逐渐占据了我的心。这种感觉变得如此强烈，以至于我决定放下所有的工作来满足我的渴望。但是我发现离开实验室不过是异想天开。几个月过去，在此期间我成功地恢复了1892年春天之前的所有记忆。在脑海被遗忘的迷雾中浮现了这样的画面：在巴黎的和平酒店，我刚从疲劳的昏睡中苏醒。有人送来一封急件，急件中写有我母亲即将去世的悲伤消息，这让我悲痛万分。我立刻动身，一路长途跋涉回到家中。母亲在数周的疾病折磨之后与世长辞！尤其值得注意的是，在记忆恢复这段时间里，我对与我的研究主题相关的一切都充满活力。我可以回忆起我实验中最微不足道的细节和无足轻重的观察结果，甚至可以背诵几页文字和复杂的数学公式。

那些平庸之辈

我坚信付出必有回报，真正的回报永远与付出的劳动和牺牲成正比。因此，可以肯定的是，在我所有的发明中，放大发射器将是对后代最重要和最有价值的，这将会得到证明，因为我为之付出得最多。放大发射器不但会带来的商业和工业革命的思考，而且会引起人们对许多工业成就的人道主义后果的反思。与文明的更高利益相比，仅考虑效用显得微不足道。我们面临的危机，不能仅仅通过物质手段来解决，无论多么富有都无济于事。不但如此，物质方面的进步充满了危险，不亚于物质匮乏带来的痛苦。如果我们要释放原子的能量，或在全球任何地方发现其他开发廉价和无限能量的方法，也许成就非凡，但这不是福气，反而可能给人类带来灾难，引发分歧和无政府状态，最终将导致暴力政权上台。最大的善意来自趋于统一和谐的技术改进——我的无线发射器就是这样。通过这种方式，人类可将声音和图像传送复制到任何地方。工厂将由数千英里^①之外的

---

① 1000 英里约等于 1609 千米。

瀑布提供电力；空中机器将不间断地在地球周围推进，并控制太阳的能量来创造湖泊和河流，将干旱的沙漠变成肥沃的土地。它用于电报、电话和类似用途，将自动消除目前对无线应用中的静电干扰和所有其他干扰。

这个话题很好，倒是可以说几句。

在过去的十年中，许多人傲慢地声称他们已经成功地消除了无线电应用中的难题。其实，这纯属胡言乱语。在他们见诸报端之前，我已经仔细检查了他们所说的大部分"解决的难题"，发现他们一个也没有解决。美国海军最近发表的一份官方声明，这或许能教会了一些容易上当的新闻编辑如何评估这些大言不惭的公告的真伪。毫无例外，这些解决难题的尝试都是基于非常荒谬的理论，无异于痴人说梦。这类消息无意中闯入我的视野时，我就会自动"打假"。就在最近，伴随铺天盖地的吹捧，宣布了一项所谓的"新发现"，没过多久就发现是一幕闹剧。

这让我想起了几年前发生的一件激动人心的事件，当时我正在用高频电流进行实验，史蒂夫·布罗迪刚刚从布鲁克林大桥跳下去。消息传到纽约，人们兴奋不已。这一壮举被后来者纷纷模仿，后来也就庸俗不堪。

那时我印象非常深刻，经常谈到史蒂夫·布罗迪这位勇敢的印刷工。在一个炎热的下午，我感到有必要搞点儿恶作剧提神醒脑。于是，我走进这座大城市很受欢迎的一家休闲餐厅，受欢迎程度全市排名应该在前三万名之内，那里提供一种美味的饮料——现在只有欧洲最贫穷和受灾的国家才能喝到。餐厅里热闹非凡，但都是平庸之辈，没有任何判断力。于是，在讨论了一件事情时，我漫不经心地说了一句："这是我跳下桥时所说的话。"我刚说出这些话，就感觉自己像是席勒诗中提到的摩太的同伴。刹那间，现场一片混乱，十几个声音喊道："是布罗迪！"我往柜台上扔了 25 美分硬币，然后冲向门口，但人群紧跟在我身后大喊："站住，史蒂夫！"当我疯狂地奔向藏身之处时，许多人对我围追堵截，他们把我当成了史蒂夫·布罗迪。幸运的是，我在拐角处飞奔——通过消防通道逃跑，回到了实验室。我脱掉了外套，操起铁锤，伪装成一个勤劳的铁匠，叮叮当当开始了锻造。但事实证明，这些伪装是多余的，他们根本追不到这里来。多年后的夜里，当想象变成幻觉，当白天的琐事在眼前飘过时，我经常在床上翻来覆去想，如果那群人抓住了我，发现我不是史蒂夫·布罗迪，会怎么对待我？

消除干扰

如今，有位工程师最近在一个技术机构宣称有种新方法可以消除静电，这种方法基于"迄今为止未知的自然法则"。他信口开河，称把地面和大气层之上当成一个巨大的电容器，用一种方式让这个电容器充放电，静电干扰就在竖直方向上振动，而发射器的信号就能沿水平方向沿地球表面传播，不再受干扰影响。这种充放电可以消除干扰？这完全违背了物理学讲义。就算在富兰克林的时代，这种假设也会被谴责为信口开河。因为与此有关的事实当时是众所周知的，大气中的电与机器产生的电是同样的电。所以显而易见的是，自然产生的静电干扰和机器产生的电信号以完全相同的方式在地球和空气中传播，并且都在水平方向和垂直方向上产生电动势，用那个方法肯定不能把它们分开。任何此类方法都无法克服干扰。事实是这样的：在空气中，电势以每英尺①高度约 50 伏的梯度增加，因此在空气的上端和下端之间可能存在 20 伏甚至 4 万伏的压差。带电大气的不断运动并向导体释放电流，这种放电不是连续的而是

① 1 英尺等于 0.3048 米。

破坏性的，这会在敏感的电话接收器中产生刺啦刺啦的摩擦声。天线越高，电线所包围的空间越大，效果越明显，但必须理解，它纯粹是局部的，与真正的麻烦关系不大。

1900年，在完善我的无线系统时，有种设备包含4个天线。这些都经过仔细校准到相同的频率，并对接收的信号多重连接，实现从任何方向接收并放大。当我想确定传输信号的来源时，每个对角天线对都与一个作为检测器的初级线圈串联，初级线圈给检测器供电。在前一种情况下，电话里的声音很大；在后者中，没有声音，正如预期的那样，两个对角相互抵消，但两种情况下都显示有静电，我不得不设计体现不同原理的装置以清除静电干扰。

通过接地有可能解决问题。正如我很久以前所建议的那样，接地可以消除现在建造的建筑物中非常严重的由带电空气引起的问题，此外，各种静电干扰也会因接地而衰减，由于电路的方向性，而静电干扰来自四面八方，差不多能衰减到原来的一半。这是完全不言而喻的，但对于一些头脑简单的无线电爱好者来说，这是一个新的启示。他们的经验过于简单，能想到设备改进差不多用斧头就可以完成，因为他们只关注表面，根本不知道实际上发生了什么。如果实际干扰来自空中，那么只要不把天线架在空中，干扰问题就不复存在。但是，事实上根本不是这么回事。按照这种观点，埋在地下的电线应该是绝对没问题，但实验证明它比架在空中的电线更容易受到某些外来脉冲的影响。公平地说，已经取得了一些进展，但不是通过任何特定的方法或设备。它是简单地通过扔掉那些差劲而没用的结构，换上更合适的接收器来实现的。正如我在上一篇文章中指出的，要彻底解决这个困难，必须对系统进行彻底的改变，而且越早越好。

无线电转输

事实上，如果无线电传输在起步阶段并且绝大多数人（甚至专家）对它的最终可能性没有概念的时候，立法机关会匆忙通过一项措施，使其成为政府垄断，那将是灾难性的。这是丹尼尔部长 [1] 几周前提出的，毫无疑问，这位杰出的官员以真诚的信念向参议院和众议院提出了议案。但普遍的证据明确无误地表明，最好的结果

---

[1] 丹尼尔·约瑟夫斯 1913—1921 年任美国海军部长。

总是在健康的商业竞争中获得。然而，无线网络应该被赋予最大的发展自由是有特殊原因的。首先，与人类历史上的任何其他发明或发现相比，它为改善人类生活提供了不可估量的更大和更重要的前景。还有，必须理解的是，这种奇妙的艺术已经在这里完整地发展起来，与电话、白炽灯或飞机相比，称其为"美国化"更恰当和得体。有进取心的新闻代理人和股票经纪人在传播错误信息方面非常成功，即使是《科学美国人》这样优秀的期刊也将主要功劳归于国外。当然，德国人赫兹验证了电磁波，而俄罗斯、英国、法国和意大利的专家很快就将它们用于信号传输目的。这是新技术的明显应用，并通过旧的经典的、未经改进的感应线圈完成——其重要性与发现小孔成像差不多。传输半径非常有限，所获得的结果没有什么价值，而电磁波作为一种传递情报的手段，本可以被我在1891年倡导的声波所取代。而且，所有这些尝试都是在今天普遍采用的无线系统的基本原理提出三年之后进行的，它的强大效能在美国得到了清晰的描述和发展。那些赫兹的设备和方法的踪迹现在已不复存在。我们朝着完全相反的方向前进，所做的是这个国家公民的智慧和努力的产物。基础专利已过期，机会向所有人开放。部长先生的主要论点是基于干扰。据《纽约先驱报》7月29日报道，他的声明称，来自强大电台的信号可以在世界每个村庄被截获。鉴于我在1900年的实验中证明的这一事实，仅在美国加以限制并没有什么意义。

为了阐明这一点，我可以提一下，就在最近，一位长相古怪的绅士拜访了我，目的是争取我的帮助，在某个遥远的土地上建造世界发射器。"我们没有钱，"他说，"只一车金条，你拿多少都行。"我告诉他，我想先看看我的发明在美国会做什么，会面就这样结束了。但我很满意一些看不见的力量在起作用，随着时间的推移，维持不间断的通信将变得更加困难，唯一的补救办法是系统不受干扰。其实它已经存在，并且很完善，所需要的只是将它投入使用。

世界上可怕的冲突仍然是最重要的存在，也许放大发射器可以作为攻击和防御的机器，尤其是远程控制的使用。这项发明是从我童年开始并持续一生的观察的合乎逻辑的结果。当第一个结果发表时，《电气评论》社论称它将成为"推动人类进步和文明的最有力元素之一"。实现这一预言的时间并不遥远。在1898年和1900年，它被提供给政府，如果我像其他人一样会阿谀奉承，这项发明可能早就被采纳了。当时，我真的认为它能消灭战争，因为它具有巨大的破坏性，而且不必让人到前线作战。然而，虽然我并没有对它的潜力失去信心，但我的观点从那以后发生了变化。

除非消除下一次战争发生的原因，否则战争不可避免。归根结底，战争是我们生活的星球的组成部分。只有在各方面消除距离障碍，实现信息的传递、乘客和物资的运输以及能源的传输，才能确保各国友好关系的持久性。我们现在最想要的是世界各地的个人和社区之间更密切的联系和更好的沟通，以及消除对过度拔高民族主义的自私自利和极度自负的理想的狂热追捧，这种理想总是容易使世界陷入原始的野蛮和冲突。任何联盟或议会采用任何手段都不能阻止这样的灾难。这些只是将弱者置于强者手中的新手段。十四年前，我曾在这方面表达过自己的这个观点。当时，已故的安德鲁·卡内基提出了几个主要政府的组合（一种联盟），在总统的努力之前就有很大的推动，并提供了宣传推广。虽然不能否认这样的协定可能对一些不幸的民族带来真正的好处，但它并不能达到所寻求的主要目标。和平只能作为大众启蒙和种族融合的自然结果而出现，我们离这种幸福的实现还很远。

当我审视当今世界时，鉴于我们目睹的剧烈的对抗与战争，我坚信如果美国保持其传统并远离"纠缠联盟"，大众的利益将得到最好的服务。这个国家在地理上独特而优越：远离一触即发的战争之地，没有扩张领土的动机，拥有取之不尽的资源和浸淫着自由和权利精神的庞大人口。因此，美国能够独立地发挥其巨大的力量和道德力量来造福所有人，比作为一个联盟的成员更明智和有效。

在《电气实验者》上发表的其中一篇传记中，我详述了我早年的生活环境，并讲述了一种痛苦，它迫使我坚持不懈地运用想象力和自我观察。这种心理活动，起初在疾病和痛苦的压力下是非自愿的，逐渐成为第二天性，并最终让我认识到我只是一个没有思想和行动、没有自由意志的"机器人"，只会对环境做出反应。我们的身体结构如此复杂，我们进行的动作如此繁多，外部给我们感官的印象如此微妙和难以捉摸，以至于一般人很难掌握这一事实。然而，对于受过训练的研究人员来说，没有什么比300年前笛卡尔在一定程度上理解和提出的生命力学理论更有说服力了。但在他那个时代，我们有机体的许多重要功能是未知的，特别是关于光的性质以及眼睛的构造和运作，哲学家们一无所知。

近年来，这些领域的科学研究进展之快，已发表了许多著作，这一观点已不容置疑。它最能干和最有说服力的代表之一也许是巴斯德的前助手费利克斯·勒·丹泰克。雅克·洛布教授在日光性方面进行了引起关注的实验，清楚地展示了低等生物体中的光的力量，他的最新著作《强制运动》具有启发性。但是，尽管科学界人士也接受这一理论，就像其他任何公认的理论一样，但对我来说，这是一个真理，我时时刻刻都通过我的行动和思想来证明。对外部印象的意识促使我进行任何形式的体力或精神上的努力，这种意识一直存在于我的脑海中。只有在罕见的情况下，当我处于异常专注的状态时，最初的冲动才不那么明显。

迄今为止，更多的人从未意识到他们周围和内部正在传递什么，数以百万计的人因此成为疾病的受害者并过早死亡。在他们看来，最常见的日常事件显得神秘莫测。云朵遮住太阳再正常不过，但有人可能会感到悲伤，绞尽脑汁寻求解释，就算他可能已经注意到原因也无济于事。他在街上遇到了朋友，或在某处看到朋友的照片，他可能会"真的"看到他亲爱的朋友的形象。当他失去领扣时，他大惊小怪，咒骂了一个小时，无法想象自己以前的动作并直接定位对象。缺乏观察只是一种无知，是导致许多病态观念和愚蠢想法流行的原因。不超过十分之一的人否定心灵感应和其他精神表现，否定招魂术和与死者的交流，并且拒绝倾听相关人员的陈述。

为了说明这种趋势在头脑清醒的美国民众中根深蒂固，我可能会提到一个滑稽的事件。

战前不久，当我在这座城市展出的涡轮机在技术论文中引起广泛评论时，我预计会有制造商争夺发明权，我特别关注来自底特律的那个人，他拥有积累数百万美元的不可思议的能力。我对他在某一天会出现非常有信心，我向我的秘书和助手肯定地宣布。果然，一个晴朗的早晨，福特汽车公司的一群工程师提出与我讨论一个重要项目的请求。"我说得没错吧？"我得意扬扬地对我的员工们说。其中一位员工说："特斯拉先生，你真了不起；一切都如你所料。"当这些顽固的人坐下时，我当然立即开始赞美我的涡轮机的美妙特性，这时发言人打断了我说："我们知道这一切，但我们正在执行一项特殊任务。我们已经成立了一个研究精神现象的心理学协会，我们希望你能加入我们的行列。"那个时刻，我窘迫极了，真希望我的员工们不在现场。

"超自然"的事件

自从那个时代的一些最伟大的人、名字不朽的科学领袖告诉我，我拥有一个不寻常的头脑，我不惜牺牲所有的思维能力来解决重大问题。多年来，我一直致力于解开死亡之谜，并热切地观察着各种灵性迹象。但在我的人生过程中，我只有一次经历过让我瞬间觉得算得上是超自然的经历。那是在我母亲去世的时候。我已经被痛苦和长期的警觉彻底耗尽，一天晚上被带到离我们家大约两个街区的一栋楼里。当我无助地躺在那里时，我想如果我母亲在我不在她床边的时候去世，她一定会给我一个信号。两三个月前，我和已故的朋友威廉·克鲁克斯爵士一起在伦敦，当时讨论了招魂术，而我完全被这些想法所左右。我可能没有关注过其他人，但受到他的论点的影响，因为我在学生时代读过他的关于辐射物质的划时代著作让我接受了电气事业。我想，此刻是探索"超自然"现象最有利的条件，因为我母亲是一位天才女性，特别擅长直觉。整个晚上，我大脑中的每一根神经都在期待中绷紧，但直到清晨，我睡着了，或者可能是在半睡半醒之际，看到一朵云彩带着几个天使般美丽的身影飘然而来，其中一个慈爱地凝视着我，逐渐呈现出我母亲的容貌。她缓缓飘过房间，消失不见，我被一首难以形容的甜美的歌声惊醒。就在那一刻，一种无法用言语表达的确定性向我袭来：我的母亲刚刚去世。事情的确如此。我无法理解我预先收到的这一痛苦的消息。虽然心情沉重无比而且健康不佳，我还是给威廉·克鲁克斯爵士写了一封信。当我康复后，我花了很长时间寻找这种奇怪现象的外部原因，令我欣慰的是，经过几个月看不到希望的努力，我终于成功了。我曾看过一位著名画家的画，以云的形式寓意一个季节，一群天使似乎真的飘浮在空中，这让我印象深刻。和我梦里出现的一模一样，除了我母亲的样子。音乐是复活节清晨附近教堂的唱诗班做弥撒时传来的。按照科学事实令人满意地解释了一切。

这是很久以前的事了，从那以后，我再也没有最微弱的理由改变我对精神和精神现象的看法。相信这些是智力发展的自然产物。宗教教条的正统意义不再被接受，但每个人都坚信某种至高无上的力量。我们都必须有一个理想来管理我们的行为并确保满足，但它是信条、艺术、科学还是其他任何东西都无关紧要，只要它履行非物质化力量的功能即可。一个共同的观念应占主导地位，这对于整个人类的和平存在至关重要。

虽然我未能获得任何证据来支持心理学家和招魂师的论点，但我已经完全满意地证明了生活的自动性，不仅通过对个人行为的持续观察，而且通过某些概括更确凿地证明了这一点。这是我认为人类社会最伟大的一个发现，我将简要地谈一谈。当我非常年轻时，我第一次意识到了这个惊人的事实，但多年来只是用"巧合"来解释。事实是，每当我自己或我所依附的人，或我所致力于的事业，以一种特定的方式受到他人的伤害，这可能最普遍地被描述为最不公平的现象，我经历了一种奇异的和无法定义的痛苦，因为找不到更好的词，我称之为"天降之苦"。不久之后，那些让我痛苦的人总是悲痛欲绝。在经历了许多这样的案例之后，我把这件事告诉了一些朋友，他们或许相信我逐渐形成的理论的真实性。这个理论可能用以下几句话来概括。

我们的身体具有相似的结构，并暴露于相同的外部影响之下。这导致我们所有社会和其他规则和法律所依据的一般活动的相似性和一致性。我们是完全被介质的力量控制的自动机，就像大海上随波逐流的小舟被抛来抛去，但却把来自外部的冲动的结果误认为是自由意志。我们所做的动作和其他活动总是可以保护我们生存下去，虽然看起来彼此完全独立，但我们通过无形的联系而联系在一起。只要有机体处于完美的状态，它就会对驱动它的因素做出准确的反应，但是一旦有个体出现某种精神错乱，他的自我保护能力就会受损。当然，每个人都知道，如果一个人耳聋、视力减弱或四肢受伤，他继续存在的机会就会减少。但一个真实的情况是，也许更真实，大脑中的某些缺陷或多或少地剥夺了自动机的某种重要功能并导致它易于损坏。一个非常敏感和观察力强的人，他的高度发达的机制都完好无损，并根据环境的变化条件精确地行动，具有超越机械的感觉，使他能够避开过于微妙而无法直接感知的危险。当他接触到其他控制器官严重失灵的人时，这种感觉就会出现，他会感受到"天降之苦"。这个事实已经在数百个实例中得到证实，我请其他自然学科的学生关注这个主题，相信通过联合和系统的努力，将会获得对世界具有不可估量价值的成果。

自动机器

为了证明我的理论，建造一个无线控制的想法很早就有了，但我直到1893年才开始积极地工作，那时我开始了无线研究。在接下来的两三年里，我制造了一些可以远距离驱动的机制，并在我的实验室向参观者展示。在1896年，我设计了一台能够进行多种操作的完整机器——无线电控制船，但直到1897年年底才完工。关于这艘船，我在1900年6月的《世纪》杂志一篇文章和其他文章中进行了说明和描述。

特斯拉展示了1898年11月8日的无线电控制船（摘自1900年6月《世纪》杂志）。

当机器在1898年年初首次亮相时，它引起了我的其他发明所没有的轰动。1898年11月，在考察官来到纽约并见证了表演之后，我才获得了一项关于新技术的基本专利，因为我声称的事情太难以置信了。我记得后来我拜访了华盛顿的一位官员，希望将这项发明提供给政府，当我告诉他我的成就时，他大笑起来，因为那时还没有人相信我真的发明出那样的东西。不幸的是，在本专利中，根据我的律师的建议，我表示这是通过单个电路和一种众所周知的检测器来实现的，因为我还没有申请专利保护这个方法和装置。事实上，我的船是通过几个电路的联合作用来控制的，排除了各种干扰。大多数情况下，我采用包括冷凝器在内的回路形式的接收电路，因为我的高压发射器的放电使大厅中的空气电离，因此即使是非常小的天线也会从周围的大气中汲取电荷数小时。举个例子，我发现，例如一个直径为12英寸[①]的灯泡，快要报废了，仅有的单个端子接了一根短电线，可以连续闪烁一千次，直到实验室中的空气中的电量被中和。接收器的环路形式对这种干扰不敏感，奇怪的是它在最近这个时候变得流行起来。实际上，它收集的能量比天线或长接地线少得多，但它恰好消除了当前无线设备固有的许多缺陷。

---

① 12英寸等于30.48厘米。

在向观众展示我的发明时，参观者可以提出任何问题，无论涉及什么，自动机会用符号回答他们。这在当时被认为是魔术，但实际上非常简单，因为是我自己通过遥控设备给出了回复。

在同一时期，建造了另一艘更大的遥控船，它的一张照片展示在这期的《电气实验员》之中。它由线圈控制，在船体中放置了几圈，完全防水并且能够下潜。该设备与第一个设备相似，除了我引入的某些特殊功能，例如白炽灯，它提供了机器正常运行的可见证据。

然而，这些自动机控制在操作员的视野范围内，是我所设想的远程自动机艺术发展的第一步，也是相当粗略的步骤。下一个合乎逻辑的改进是将其应用于超出视野范围和远离控制中心的自动机制，从那时起，我一直主张将它们用作战争工具，优先于枪支。现在看来，这一点的重要性已经得到承认。如果我要从媒体上的随意宣布来判断的话，这些成就被认为是非凡的，但无论如何没有任何新奇之处。以一种不完善的方式，利用现有的无线设备，发射一架飞机，让它遵循一定的近似航线，并在数百英里^①的距离上执行一些操作是可行的。

---

① 100 英里约为 160.9 千米。

这种机器也可以通过多种方式进行机械控制，我毫不怀疑它可能在战争中证明是有用的。但是，据我所知，今天没有任何工具可以精确地实现这样的目标。我在这件事上投入了多年的研究，并发展了一些工具，使这样和更大的奇迹很容易实现。

如前所述，当我还是一名大学生时，我构想了一种与现在完全不同的飞行器。基本原则是合理的，但由于缺乏足够强的发动机而无法付诸实践。近年来，我已经成功地解决了这个问题，现在正在计划没有机翼、副翼、螺旋桨和其他外部附件的飞行器，这些飞行器将具有极高的速度，很可能在不久的将来为和平提供有力的保护。这种完全由反作用力维持和推动的机器，应该由机械或无线能量控制。通过安装适当的装置，将这种飞行器（携带炸弹）发射到空中并将其几乎落在指定地点（可能在数千英里[①]外）将是切实可行的。但我们不会就此止步，更加自动的机械最终将被生产出来，能够像拥有自己的智慧一样行事，它们的出现将引发一场革命。早在1898年，我就向一家大型制造企业的代表提议建造和公开展示一辆汽车车厢，让其自行执行各种类似于判断的操

[①] 1000 英里约等于 1609 千米。

作。但当时我的提议被认为是空想，没有任何结果。

目前，许多最有能力的人正试图设计权宜之计，以防止可怕的战争再次发生，这种冲突的终结只是理论上的，而我在 1914 年 12 月 20 日发表在《太阳报》上的一篇文章中正确预测了这种冲突的持续时间和主要问题。所提议的联盟不是一种补救措施，但相反，在一些有能力的人看来，可能会带来相反的结果。尤其令人遗憾的是，在制定和平条款时采取了惩罚性政策，因为几年后，各国将有可能在没有军队、船只或枪支的情况下，而是使用更可怕的武器进行破坏，范围几乎没有限制。一座城市，无论离敌人有多远，都可以被摧毁，地球上没有任何力量可以阻止。如果我们想避免即将发生的灾难和可能将地球变成地狱的状态，我们应该毫不迟疑地以国家的全部力量和资源推动飞行器和无线能量传输的发展。

特斯拉年表

1856 年	尼古拉·特斯拉出生在奥匈帝国的斯米连村的一个塞尔维亚家庭，现位于克罗地亚境内。
1862 年	6 岁，特斯拉一家搬到戈斯皮奇，在那里完成了小学教育和初级实科中学的教育。
1863 年	7 岁，特斯拉的哥哥骑马意外坠亡。
1870 年	14 岁，特斯拉寄居在克罗地亚卡尔洛瓦茨的姨妈家里，完成了高级实科中学的教育。
1873 年	17 岁，特斯拉不顾父亲的反对返回戈斯皮奇，结果感染了霍乱，卧床 9 个月。带来的一个后果就是父亲允许他去学理工，而不是神学。
1874 年	18 岁，特斯拉康复之后逃避了兵役，根据父亲的建议，带着一捆书四海云游。
1875 年	19 岁，特斯拉就读位于格拉茨的理工大学。第一年积极学习并参加演讲，创建了塞尔维亚文化俱乐部。

1876 年	20 岁，与教授因无刷电机是否可能而发生冲突，失去奖学金并开始赌博。
1877 年	21 岁，特斯拉不再听课。
1878 年	22 岁，辍学。离开奥地利，到斯洛文尼亚的马里博尔，在一家工程公司当绘图员。在酒吧里下棋、打牌。
1879 年	23 岁，因没有居留许可，被遣返回戈斯皮奇。
1880 年	24 岁，到达布拉格，准备进入查尔斯大学（即后来的布拉格大学）读书，因不懂希腊语，大部分时间在图书馆与咖啡馆度过。听过大学的讲座，但没有分数。
1881 年	25 岁，在叔叔的安排下到匈牙利正在建设中的布达佩斯电话交流中心工作，发现无法开展工作转而到中央电报局当制图员。几个月后，电话交流中心建成，特斯拉成为首席电工，多次改善设备，并发明了放大器。
1882 年	26 岁，痴迷于交流电，精神崩溃。恢复后，在布达佩斯散步时，想到《浮士德》的诗，豁然开朗，问题得以解决。
1883 年	27 岁，受大陆爱迪生公司的委托，特斯拉到法国斯特拉斯堡修理并安装在德国铁路公司的新直流电照明系统。这个系统在试运行时就出故障损坏了。
1884 年	28 岁，在叔叔的资助下乘船前往美国纽约，进入爱迪生的公司工作。后来对薪酬不满意离开。
1885 年	29 岁，找到投资者，成立特斯拉电灯公司。在完成技术难题后，被迫离开公司。

| **1886 年** | 30 岁，为了生计做"挖沟工"，经历了人生黑暗时刻。 |

| **1887 年** | 31 岁，西联的董事与纽约的一位律师投资交流电系统。特斯拉获得了资金。 |

| **1888 年** | 32 岁，在纽约哥伦比亚大学的美国电气工程师协会发表有关交流电及电力传送的演讲。 |

| **1889 年** | 33 岁，在纽约格兰德街 175 号建立新的实验室。 |

| **1890 年** | 34 岁，凭借高频设备，开发了霓虹灯、荧光管，并开启了无线传输的研究。 |

| **1891 年** | 35 岁，在纽约哥伦比亚大学的美国电气工程师协会发表有关超高频交流电的演讲。 |

| **1892 年** | 36 岁，在伦敦做有关高压高频电流的报告。 |

| **1893 年** | 37 岁，在费城做有关光与高频的报告。 |

| **1895 年** | 39 岁，大火烧毁了实验室。数百个发明模型及大量的笔记、照片、工具被烧毁。 |

| **1896 年** | 40 岁，参观了尼亚加拉大瀑布的发电站。 |

| **1899 年** | 43 岁，约翰·雅各布·阿斯特为特斯拉投资了巨资用于改进照明系统，成为特斯拉最大的投资者，但特斯拉把资金用在了科罗拉多的实验之中。两人因此出现隔阂。后来阿斯特在"泰坦尼克"号沉没时遇难。 |

| **1901 年** | 45 岁，与摩根大通签订了专利转让的协议。 |

1910 年	54 岁，涡轮机取得成功，将办公室搬到大都会大厦。
1915 年	59 岁，传闻拒绝和爱迪生分享诺贝尔奖而导致奖项另选他人。
1916 年	60 岁，陷入债务危机，身无分文。
1917 年	61 岁，获"爱迪生奖章"。
1919 年	63 岁，开始写自传。
1924 年	68 岁，因欠酒店费用而被起诉。
1930 年	74 岁，由朋友及仰慕者还清债务，并让他搬到新的酒店。
1931 年	75 岁，收到了爱因斯坦等著名科学家的贺信。
1934 年	78 岁，西屋电气向特斯拉支付费用，并为他租了永久性酒店。
1943 年	1 月 7 日，86 岁（不满 87 岁），特斯拉逝世于纽约市纽约客酒店 33 层 3327 号房间。

译后记

尼古拉·特斯拉在交流电领域成就非凡，在世界上留下了深刻的印记。在翻译过程中，我更注重意译而非直译，以确保读者能够顺畅理解并且沉浸其中。翻译此书，就像踏上一段奇妙的旅程，时常进入沉思，回味无穷。在此，我分享翻译此书的一些感想与收获。

特斯拉能将脑海中的景象"投影"在眼前，能甩出飞石把跃出水面的鱼儿断为两半，似乎拥有诸多的不可思议的技能。但这并不是我关注的重点。在当今的网络视频平台上，我们可以看到许多神通广大的人才，能用单手倒立，能飞檐走壁，甚至能腾空翻过几米宽的水面。特斯拉与他们有什么不同呢？不同之处在于特斯拉改变了世界！他不仅仅是一个成功的发明家和科学家，更是一个改变世界的梦想家！他的追求并不局限于个人的成就，而是致力于推动科学技术的发展和人类社会的进步。因为特斯拉，我们的世界与之前不再相同。

改变世界需要巨大的力量，这种力量首先来自特斯拉对创造性思维活动的热爱。特斯拉想做自己喜欢的事情并不容易，最大的阻碍来自于他的父亲。经历诸多波折，特斯拉最终如愿以偿。这让我想到陶行知先生的诗："人生天地间，各自有秉赋。为一大事来，做一大事去。多少白发翁，蹉跎悔歧路。寄语少年人，莫将少年误。"特斯拉的故事验证了一句话：唯有热爱，方能卓越。没有热爱的科学发现和技术创新是不可想象的，改变世界也是不可能的。

读书或许是特斯拉成功的另一秘诀。书中提到，特斯拉读书如痴如醉，通宵达旦。对特斯拉来说，读书不只是丰富了知识。他在病中读书，能"起死回生"；他在遇到技术瓶颈时读书，能恍然大悟，醍醐灌顶。以特斯拉的智慧和能量都需要如此读书，那作为平凡的人应该如何做也就不言而喻了。另外，读书唤醒了特斯拉的意志力，实现了极强的自我控制，这种自我控制让特斯拉尝到了"甜头"，一发而不可收拾。在他人看起来无法办到的事情，对特斯拉来说却轻而易举。

总体来说，特斯拉的影响力不仅限于科学和技术领域，他的创造力和追求卓越的精神激励着一代又一代的科学家、工程师和创新者，也鼓舞着人们勇敢地追求自己的梦想，点亮灿烂的人生！

译　者

2023 年 5 月 5 日

My Inventions

The Autobiography of Nikola Tesla

First published in 1919

Chapter 1

————◆·※·◆————

My Early Life

The progressive development of man is vitally dependent on invention. It is the most important product of his creative brain. Its ultimate purpose is the complete mastery of mind over the material world, the harnessing of the forces of nature to human needs. This is the difficult task of the inventor who is often misunderstood and unrewarded. But he finds ample compensation in the pleasing exercises of his powers and in the knowledge of being one of that exceptionally privileged class without whom the race would have long ago perished in the bitter struggle against pitiless elements.

---

* 为了阅读方便，编者把个别词的拼写做了调整，更符合现代的拼写习惯。

Speaking for myself, I have already had more than my full measure of this exquisite enjoyment, so much that for many years my life was little short of continuous rapture. I am credited with being one of the hardest workers and perhaps I am, if thought is the equivalent of labor, for I have devoted to it almost all of my waking hours. But if work is interpreted to be a definite performance in a specified time according to a rigid rule, then I may be the worst of idlers. Every effort under compulsion demands a sacrifice of life-energy. I never paid such a price. On the contrary, I have thrived on my thoughts.

In attempting to give a connected and faithful account of my activities in this series of articles which will be presented with the assistance of the Editors of the ELECTRICAL EXPERIMENTER and are chiefly addressed to our young men readers, I must dwell, however reluctantly, on the impressions of my youth and the circumstances and events which have been instrumental in determining my career.

Our first endeavors are purely instinctive, promptings of an imagination vivid and undisciplined. As we grow older reason asserts itself and we become more and more systematic and designing. But those early impulses, tho not immediately productive, are of the greatest moment and may shape our very destinies. Indeed, I feel now that had I understood and cultivated instead of suppressing them, I would have added substantial value to my bequest to the world. But not until I had attained manhood did I realize that I was an inventor.

This was due to a number of causes. In the first place I had a brother who was gifted to an extraordinary degree— one of those rare phenomena of mentality which biological investigation has failed to explain. His premature death left my parents disconsolate. We owned a horse which had been presented to us by a dear friend. It was a magnificent animal of Arabian breed, possessed of almost human intelligence, and was cared for and petted by the whole family, having on one occasion saved my father's life under remarkable circumstances. My father had been called one winter night to perform an urgent duty and while crossing the mountains, infested by wolves, the horse became frightened and ran away, throwing him violently to the ground. It arrived home bleeding and exhausted, but after the alarm was sounded immediately dashed off again, returning to the spot, and before the searching party were far on the way they were met by my father, who had recovered consciousness and remounted, not realizing that he had been lying in the snow for several hours. This horse was responsible for my brother's injuries from which he died. I witnessed the tragic scene and altho fifty- six years have elapsed since, my visual impression of it has lost none of its force. The recollection of his attainments made every effort of mine seem dull in comparison.

Anything I did that was creditable merely caused my parents to feel their loss more keenly. So I grew up with little confidence in myself. But I was far from being considered a stupid boy, if I am to judge from an incident of which I have still a strong remembrance. One day the Aldermen were passing thru a street where I was at play with other boys. The oldest of these venerable gentlemen— a wealthy citizen—paused to give a silver piece to each of us. Coming to me he suddenly stopt and commanded, "Look in my eyes." I met his gaze, my hand outstretched to receive the much valued coin, when, to my dismay, he said,

"No, not much, you can get nothing from me, you are too smart." They used to tell a funny story about me. I had two old aunts with wrinkled faces, one of them having two teeth protruding like the tusks of an elephant which she buried in my cheek every time she kissed me. Nothing would scare me more than the prospect of being hugged by these as affectionate as unattractive relatives. It happened that while being carried in my mother's arms they asked me who was the prettier of the two. After examining their faces intently, I answered thoughtfully, pointing to one of them, "This here is not as ugly as the other."

Then again, I was intended from my very birth for the clerical profession and this thought constantly oppressed me. I longed to be an engineer but my father was inflexible. He was the son of an officer who served in the army of the Great Napoleon and, in common with his brother, professor of mathematics in a prominent institution, had received a military education but, singularly enough, later embraced the clergy in which vocation he achieved eminence. He was a very erudite man, a veritable natural philosopher, poet and writer and his sermons were said to be as eloquent as those of Abraham a Sancta-Clara. He had a prodigious memory and frequently recited at length from works in several languages. He often remarked playfully that if some of the classics were lost he could restore them. His style of writing was much admired. He penned sentences short and terse and was full of wit and satire. The humorous remarks he made were always peculiar and characteristic. Just to illustrate, I may mention one or two instances. Among the help there was a cross-eyed man called Mane, employed to do work around the farm. He was chopping wood one day. As he swung the axe my father, who stood nearby and felt very uncomfortable, cautioned him, "For God's sake, Mane, do not strike at what you are looking but at what you intend to hit." On another occasion he was taking out for a drive a friend who carelessly permitted his costly fur coat to rub on the carriage wheel. My father reminded him of it saying, "Pull in your coat, you are ruining my tire." He had the odd habit of talking to himself and would often carry on an animated conversation and indulge in heated argument, changing the tone of his voice. A casual listener might have sworn that several people were in the room.

Altho I must trace to my mother's influence whatever inventiveness I possess, the training he gave me must have been helpful. It comprised all sorts of exercises — as, guessing one another's thoughts, discovering the defects of some form or expression, repeating long sentences or performing mental calculations. These daily lessons were intended to strengthen memory and reason and especially to develop the critical sense, and were undoubtedly very beneficial.

My mother descended from one of the oldest families in the country and a line of inventors. Both her father and grandfather originated numerous implements for household, agricultural and other uses. She was a truly great woman, of rare skill, courage and fortitude, who had braved the storms of life and past thru many a trying experience. When she was sixteen a virulent pestilence swept the country. Her father was called away to administer the last sacraments to the dying and during his absence she went alone to the assistance of a neighboring family who were stricken by the dread disease. All of the members, five in number, succumbed in rapid succession. She bathed, clothed and laid out the bodies, decorating them with flowers according to the custom of the country and when her father returned he found everything ready for a Christian burial. My mother was an inventor of the first order and would, I believe, have achieved great things had she not been so remote from modern life and its multifold opportunities. She invented and constructed all kinds of tools and devices and wove the finest designs from thread which was spun by her. She even planted the seeds, raised the plants and separated the fibers herself. She worked indefatigably, from break of day till late at night, and most of the wearing apparel and furnishings of the home was the product of her hands. When she was past sixty, her fingers were still nimble enough to tie three knots in an eyelash.

There was another and still more important reason for my late awakening. In my boyhood I suffered from a peculiar affliction due to the appearance of images, often accompanied by strong flashes of light, which marred the sight of real objects and interfered with my thought and action. They were pictures of things and scenes which I had really seen, never of those I imagined. When a word was spoken to me the image of the object it designated would present itself vividly to my vision and sometimes I was quite unable to distinguish whether what I saw was tangible or not. This caused me great discomfort and anxiety. None of the students of psychology or physiology whom I have consulted could ever explain satisfactorily these phenomena. They seem to have been unique altho I was probably predisposed as I know that my brother experienced a similar trouble. The theory I have formulated is that the images were the result of a reflex action from the brain on the retina under great excitation. They certainly were not hallucinations such as are produced in diseased and anguished minds, for in other respects I was normal and composed. To give an idea of my distress, suppose that I had witnessed a funeral or some such nerve-racking spectacle. Then, inevitably, in the stillness of night, a vivid picture of the scene would thrust itself before my eyes and persist despite all my efforts to banish it. Sometimes it would even remain fixt in space tho I pushed my hand thru it. If my explanation is correct, it should be able to project on a screen the image of any object one conceives and make it visible. Such an advance would revolutionize all human relations. I am convinced that this wonder can and will be accomplished in time to come; I may add that I have devoted much thought to the solution of the problem.

To free myself of these tormenting appearances, I tried to concentrate my mind on something else I had seen, and in this way I would of ten obtain temporary relief; but in order to get it I had to conjure continuously new images. It was not long before I found that I had exhausted all of those at my command; my "reel" had run out, as it were, because I had seen little of the world—only objects in my home and the immediate surroundings. As I performed these mental operations for the second or third time, in order to chase the appearances from my vision, the remedy gradually lost all its force. Then I instinctively commenced to make excursions beyond the limits of the small world of which I had knowledge, and I saw new scenes. These were at first very blurred and indistinct, and would flit away when I tried to concentrate my attention upon them, but by and by I succeeded in fixing them; they gained in strength and distinctness and finally assumed the concreteness of real things. I soon discovered that my best comfort was attained if I simply went on in my vision farther and farther, getting new impressions all the time, and so I began to travel— of course, in my mind. Every night (and sometimes during the day), when alone, I would start on my journeys—see new places, cities and countries—live there, meet people and make friendships and acquaintances and, however unbelievable, it is a fact that they were just as dear to me as those in actual life and not a bit less intense in their manifestations.

This I did constantly until I was about seventeen when my thoughts turned seriously to invention. Then I observed to my delight that I could visualize with the greatest facility. I needed no models, drawings or experiments. I could picture them all as real in my mind. Thus I have been led unconsciously to evolve what I consider a new method of materializing inventive concepts and ideas, which is radically opposite to the purely experimental and is in my opinion ever so much more expeditious and efficient. The moment one constructs a device to carry into practise a crude idea he finds himself unavoidably engrossed with the details and defects of the apparatus. As he goes on improving and reconstructing, his force of concentration diminishes and he loses sight of the great underlying principle. Results may be obtained but always at the sacrifice of quality.

My method is different. I do not rush into actual work. When I get an idea I start at once building it up in my imagination. I change the construction, make improvements and operate the device in my mind. It is absolutely immaterial to me whether I run my turbine in thought or test it in my shop. I even note if it is out of balance. There is no difference whatever, the results are the same. In this way I am able to rapidly develop and perfect a conception without touching anything. When I have gone so far as to embody in the invention every possible improvement I can think of and see no fault anywhere, I put into concrete form this final product of my brain. Invariably my device works as I conceived that it should, and the experiment comes out exactly as I planned it. In twenty years there has not been a single exception. Why should it be otherwise? Engineering, electrical and mechanical, is positive in results. There is scarcely a subject that cannot be mathematically treated and the effects calculated or the results determined beforehand from the available theoretical and practical data. The carrying out into practise of a crude idea as is being generally done is, I hold, nothing but a waste of energy, money and time.

My early affliction had, however, another compensation. The incessant mental exertion developed my powers of observation and enabled me to discover a truth of great importance. I had noted that the appearance of images was always preceded by actual vision of scenes under peculiar and generally very exceptional conditions and I was impelled on each occasion to locate the original impulse. After a while this effort grew to be almost automatic and I gained great facility in connecting cause and effect. Soon I became aware, to my surprise, that every thought I conceived was suggested by an external impression. Not only this but all my actions were prompted in a similar way. In the course of time it became perfectly evident to me that I was merely an automaton endowed with power of movement, responding to the stimuli of the sense organs and thinking and acting accordingly. The practical result of this was the art of telautomatics which has been so far carried out only in an imperfect manner. Its latent possibilities will, however, be eventually shown. I have been since years planning self-controlled automata and believe that mechanisms can be produced which will act as if possessed of reason, to a limited degree, and will create a revolution in many commercial and industrial departments.

I was about twelve years old when I first succeeded in banishing an image from my vision by wilful effort, but I never had any control over the flashes of light to which I have referred. They were, perhaps, my strangest experience and inexplicable. They usually occurred when I found myself in a dangerous or distressing situation, or when I was greatly exhilarated. In some instances I have seen all the air around me filled with tongues of living flame. Their intensity, instead of diminishing, increased with time and seemingly attained a maximum when I was about twenty-five years old. While in Paris, in 1883, a prominent French manufacturer sent me an invitation to a shooting expedition which I accepted. I had been long confined to the factory and the fresh air had a wonderfully invigorating effect on me. On my return to the city that night I felt a positive sensation that my brain had caught fire. I saw a light as tho a small sun was located in it and I past the whole night applying cold compressions to my tortured head. Finally the flashes diminished in frequency and force but it took more than three weeks before they wholly subsided. When a second invitation was extended to me my answer was an emphatic NO!

These luminous phenomena still manifest themselves from time to time, as when a new idea opening up possibilities strikes me, but they are no longer exciting, being of relatively small intensity. When I close my eyes I invariably observe first, a background of very dark and uniform blue, not unlike the sky on a clear but starless night. In a few seconds this field becomes animated with innumerable scintillating flakes of green, arranged in several layers and advancing towards me. Then there appears, to the right, a beautiful pattern of two systems of parallel and closely spaced lines, at right angles to one another, in all sorts of colors with yellow-green and gold predominating. Immediately thereafter the lines grow brighter and the whole is thickly sprinkled with dots of twinkling light. This picture moves slowly across the field of vision and in about ten seconds vanishes to the left, leaving behind a ground of rather unpleasant and inert grey which quickly gives way to a billowy sea of clouds, seemingly trying to mould themselves in living shapes. It is curious that I cannot project a form into this grey until the second phase is reached. Every time, before falling asleep, images of persons or objects flit before my view. When I see them I know that I am about to lose consciousness. If they are absent and refuse to come it means a sleepless night.

To what an extent imagination played a part in my early life I may illustrate by another odd experience. Like most children I was fond of jumping and developed an intense desire to support myself in the air. Occasionally a strong wind richly charged with oxygen blew from the mountains rendering my body as light as cork and then I would leap and float in space for a long time. It was a delightful sensation and my disappointment was keen when later I undeceived myself.

During that period I contracted many strange likes, dislikes and habits, some of which I can trace to external impressions while others are unaccountable. I had a violent aversion against the earrings of women but other ornaments, as bracelets, pleased me more or less according to design. The sight of a pearl would almost give me a fit but I was fascinated with the glitter of crystals or objects with sharp edges and plane surfaces. I would not touch the hair of other people except, perhaps, at the point of a revolver. I would get a fever by looking at a peach and if a piece of camphor was anywhere in the house it caused me the keenest discomfort. Even now I am not insensible to some of these upsetting impulses. When I drop little squares of paper in a dish filled with liquid, I always sense a peculiar and awful taste in my mouth. I counted the steps in my walks and calculated the cubical contents of soup plates, coffee cups and pieces of food— otherwise my meal was unenjoyable. All repeated acts or operations I performed had to be divisible by three and if I mist I felt impelled to do it all over again, even if it took hours.

Up to the age of eight years, my character was weak and vacillating. I had neither courage or strength to form a firm resolve. My feelings came in waves and surges and vibrated unceasingly between extremes. My wishes were of consuming force and like the heads of the hydra, they multiplied. I was oppressed by thoughts of pain in life and death and religious fear. I was swayed by superstitious belief and lived in constant dread of the spirit of evil, of ghosts and ogres and other unholy monsters of the dark. Then, all at once, there came a tremendous change which altered the course of my whole existence. Of all things I liked books the best. My father had a large library and whenever I could manage I tried to satisfy my passion for reading. He did not permit it and would fly into a rage when he caught me in the act. He hid the candles when he found that I was reading in secret. He did not want me to spoil my eyes. But I obtained tallow, made the wicking and cast the sticks into tin forms, and every night I would bush the keyhole and the cracks and read, often till dawn, when all others slept and my mother started on her arduous daily task. On one occasion I came across a novel entitled "Abafi" (the Son of Aba), a Serbian translation of a well known Hungarian writer, Josika. This work somehow awakened my dormant powers of will and I began to practise self-control. At first my resolutions faded like snow in April, but in a little while I conquered my weakness and felt a pleasure I never knew before—that of doing as I willed. In the course of time this vigorous mental exercise became second nature. At the outset my wishes had to be subdued but gradually desire and will grew to be identical. After years of such discipline I gained so complete a mastery over myself that I toyed with passions which have meant destruction to some of the strongest men. At a certain age I contracted a mania for gambling which greatly worried my parents. To sit down to a game of cards was for me the quintessence of pleasure. My father led an exemplary life and could not excuse the senseless waste of time and money in which I indulged. I had a strong resolve but my philosophy was bad. I would say to him, "I can stop whenever I please but is it worth while to give up that which I would purchase with the joys of Paradise?" On frequent occasions he gave vent to his anger and contempt but my mother was different. She understood the character of men and knew that one's salvation could only be brought about thru his own efforts. One afternoon, I remember, when I had lost all my money and was craving for a game, she came to me with a roll of bills and said, "Go and enjoy yourself. The sooner you lose all we possess the better it will be. I know that you will get over it." She was right. I conquered my passion then and there and only regretted that it had not been a hundred times as strong. I not only vanquished but tore it from my heart so as not to leave even a trace of desire. Ever since that time I have been as indifferent to any form of gambling as to picking teeth.

During another period I smoked excessively, threatening to ruin my health. Then my will asserted itself and I not only stopt but destroyed all inclination. Long ago I suffered from heart trouble until I discovered that it was due to the innocent cup of coffee I consumed every morning. I discontinued at once, tho I confess it was not an easy task. In this way I checked and bridled other habits and passions and have not only preserved my life but derived an immense amount of satisfaction from what most men would consider privation and sacrifice.

After finishing the studies at the Polytechnic Institute and University I had a complete nervous breakdown and while the malady lasted I observed many phenomena strange and unbelievable.

Chapter 2

— ❖ ❆ ❖ —

My First Efforts at Invention

I shall dwell briefly on these extraordinary experiences, on account of their possible interest to students of psychology and physiology and also because this period of agony was of the greatest consequence on my mental development and subsequent labors. But it is indispensable to first relate the circumstances and conditions which preceded them and in which might be found their partial explanation.

From childhood I was compelled to concentrate attention upon myself. This caused me much suffering but, to my present view, it was a blessing in disguise for it has taught me to appreciate the inestimable value of introspection in the preservation of life, as well as a means of achievement. The pressure of occupation and the incessant stream of impressions pouring into our consciousness thru all the gateways of knowledge make modern existence hazardous in many ways. Most persons are so absorbed in the contemplation of the outside world that they are wholly oblivious to what is passing on within themselves.

The premature death of millions is primarily traceable to this cause. Even among those who exercise care it is a common mistake to avoid imaginary, and ignore the real dangers. And what is true of an individual also applies, more or less, to a people as a whole. Witness, in illustration, the prohibition movement. A drastic, if not unconstitutional, measure is now being put thru in this country to prevent the consumption of alcohol and yet it is a positive fact that coffee, tea, tobacco, chewing gum and other stimulants, which are freely indulged in even at the tender age, are vastly more injurious to the national body, judging from the number of those who succumb. So, for instance, during my student years I gathered from the published necrologues in Vienna, the home of coffee drinkers, that deaths from heart trouble sometimes reached sixty-seven per cent of the total. Similar observations might probably be made in cities where the consumption of tea is excessive. These delicious beverages superexcite and gradually exhaust the fine fibers of the brain. They also interfere seriously with arterial circulation and should be enjoyed all the more sparingly as their deleterious effects are slow and imperceptible. Tobacco, on the other hand, is conducive to easy and pleasant thinking and detracts from the intensity and concentration necessary to all original and vigorous effort of the intellect. Chewing gum is helpful for a short while but soon drains the glandular system and inflicts irreparable damage, not to speak of the revulsion it creates. Alcohol in small quantities is an excellent tonic, but is toxic in its action when absorbed in larger amounts, quite immaterial as to whether it is taken in as whiskey or produced in the stomach from sugar. But it should not be overlooked that all these are great eliminators assisting Nature, as they do, in upholding her stern but just law of the survival of the fittest. Eager reformers should also be mindful of the eternal perversity of mankind which makes the indifferent "laissez-faire" by far preferable to enforced restraint.

The truth about this is that we need stimulants to do our

best work under present living conditions, and that we must exercise moderation and control our appetites and inclinations in every direction. That is what I have been doing for many years, in this way maintaining myself young in body and mind. Abstinence was not always to my liking but I find ample reward in the agreeable experiences I am now making. Just in the hope of converting some to my precepts and convictions I will recall one or two.

A short time ago I was returning to my hotel. It was a bitter cold night, the ground slippery, and no taxi to be had. Half a block behind me followed another man, evidently as anxious as myself to get under cover. Suddenly my legs went up in the air. In the same instant there was a flash in my brain, the nerves responded, the muscles contracted, I swung thru 180 degrees and landed on my hands. I resumed my walk as tho nothing had happened when the stranger caught up with me. "How old are you?" he asked, surveying me critically. "Oh, about fifty-nine," I replied. "What of it?" "Well," said he, "I have seen a cat do this but never a man." About a month since I wanted to order new eyeglasses and went to an oculist who put me thru the usual tests. He looked at me incredulously as I read off with ease the smallest print at considerable distance. But when I told him that I was past sixty he gasped in astonishment. Friends of mine often remark that my suits fit me like gloves but they do not know that all my clothing is made to measurements which were taken nearly 35 years ago and never changed. During this same period my weight has not varied one pound.

In this connection I may tell a funny story. One evening, in the winter of 1885, Mr. Edison, Edward H. Johnson, the President of the Edison Illuminating Company, Mr. Batchellor, Manager of the works, and myself entered a little place opposite 65 Fifth Avenue where the offices of the company were located. Someone suggested guessing weights and I was induced to step on a scale. Edison felt me all over and said: "Tesla weighs 152 lbs. to an ounce," and he guest it exactly. Stript I weighed 142 lbs. and that is still my weight. I whispered to Mr. Johnson: "How is it possible that Edison could guess my weight so closely?" "Well," he said, lowering his voice. "I will tell you, confidentially, but you must not say anything. He was employed for a long time in a Chicago slaughter-house where he weighed thousands of hogs every day! That's why." My friend, the Hon. Chauncey M. Depew, tells of an Englishman on whom he sprung one of his original anecdotes and who listened with a puzzled expression but - a year later - laughed out loud. I will frankly confess it took me longer than that to appreciate Johnson's joke.

Now, my well being is simply the result of a careful and measured mode of living and perhaps the most astonishing thing is that three times in my youth I was rendered by illness a hopeless physical wreck and given up by physicians. More than this, thru ignorance and lightheartedness, I got into all sorts of difficulties, dangers and scrapes from which I extricated myself as by enchantment. I was almost drowned a dozen times; was nearly boiled alive and just mist being cremated. I was entombed, lost and frozen. I had hair-breadth escapes from mad dogs, hogs, and other wild animals. I past thru dreadful diseases and met with all kinds of odd mishaps and that I am hale and hearty today seems like a miracle. But as I recall these incidents to my mind I feel convinced that my preservation was not altogether accidental.

An inventor's endeavor is essentially lifesaving. Whether he harnesses forces, improves devices, or provides new comforts and conveniences, he is adding to the safety of our existence. He is also better qualified than the average individual to protect himself in peril, for he is observant and resourceful. If I had no other evidence that I was, in a measure, possessed of such qualities I would find it in these personal experiences. The reader will be able to judge for himself if I mention one or two instances. On one occasion, when about 14 years old, I wanted to scare some friends who were bathing with me. My plan was to dive under a long floating structure and slip out quietly at the other end. Swimming and diving came to me as naturally as to a duck and I was confident that I could perform the feat. Accordingly I plunged into the water and, when out of view, turned around and proceeded rapidly towards the opposite side. Thinking that I was safely beyond the structure, I rose to the surface but to my dismay struck a beam. Of course, I quickly dived and forged ahead with rapid strokes until my breath was beginning to give out. Rising for the second time, my head came again in contact with a beam. Now

I was becoming desperate. However, summoning all my energy, I made a third frantic attempt but the result was the same. The torture of suppressed breathing was getting unendurable, my brain was reeling and I felt myself sinking. At that moment, when my situation seemed absolutely hopeless, I experienced one of those flashes of light and the structure above me appeared before my vision. I either discerned or guest that there was a little space between the surface of the water and the boards resting on the beams and, with consciousness nearly gone, I floated up, prest my mouth close to the planks and managed to inhale a little air, unfortunately mingled with a spray of water which nearly choked me. Several times I repeated this procedure as in a dream until my heart, which was racing at a terrible rate, quieted down and I gained composure. After that I made a number of unsuccessful dives, having completely lost the sense of direction, but finally succeeded in getting out of the trap when my friends had already given me up and were fishing for my body.

That bathing season was spoiled for me thru recklessness but I soon forgot the lesson and only two years later I fell into a worse predicament. There was a large flour mill with a dam across the river near the city where I was studying at that time. As a rule the height of the water was only two or three inches above the dam and to swim out to it was a sport not very dangerous in which I often indulged. One day I went alone to the river to enjoy myself as usual. When I was a short distance from the masonry, however, I was horrified to observe that the water had risen and was carrying me along swiftly. I tried to get away but it was too late. Luckily, tho, I saved myself from being swept over by taking hold of the wall with both hands. The pressure against my chest was great and I was barely able to keep my head above the surface. Not a soul was in sight and my voice was lost in the roar of the fall. Slowly and gradually I became exhausted and unable to withstand the strain longer. just as I was about to let go, to be dashed against the rocks below, I saw in a flash of light a familiar diagram illustrating the hydraulic principle that the pressure of a fluid in motion is proportionate to the area exposed, and automatically I turned on my left side. As if by magic the pressure was reduced and I found it comparatively easy in that position to resist the force of the stream. But the danger still confronted me. I knew that sooner or later I would be carried down, as it was not possible for any help to reach me in time, even if I attracted attention. I am ambidextrous now but then I was lefthanded and had comparatively little strength in my right arm. For this reason I did not dare to turn on the other side to rest and nothing remained but to slowly push my body along the dam. I had to get away from the mill towards which my face was turned as the current there was much swifter and deeper. It was a long and painful ordeal and I came near to failing at its very end for I was confronted with a depression in the masonry. I managed to get over with the last ounce of my force and fell in a swoon when I reached the bank, where I was found. I had torn virtually all the skin from my left side and it took several weeks before the fever subsided and I was well. These are only two of many instances but they may be sufficient to show that had it not been for the inventor's instinct I would not have lived to tell this tale.

Interested people have often asked me how and when I began to invent. This I can only answer from my present recollection in the light of which the first attempt I recall was rather ambitious for it involved the invention of an apparatus and a method. In the former I was anticipated but the latter was original. It happened in this way. One of my playmates had come into the possession of a hook and fishing-tackle which created quite an excitement in the village, and the next morning all started out to catch frogs. I was left alone and deserted owing to a quarrel with this boy. I had never seen a real hook and pictured it as something wonderful, endowed with peculiar qualities, and was despairing not to be one of the party. Urged by necessity, I somehow got hold of a piece of soft iron wire, hammered the end to a sharp point between two stones, bent it into shape, and fastened it to a strong string. I then cut a rod, gathered some bait, and went down to the brook where there were frogs in abundance. But I could not catch any and was almost discouraged when it occurred to me to dangle the empty hook in front of a frog sitting on a stump. At first he collapsed but by and by his eyes bulged out and became bloodshot, he swelled to twice his normal size and made a vicious snap at the hook.

Immediately I pulled him up. I tried the same thing again and again and the method proved infallible. When my comrades, who in spite of their fine outfit had caught nothing, came to me they were green with envy. For a long time I kept my secret and enjoyed the monopoly but finally yielded to the spirit of Christmas. Every boy could then do the same and the following summer brought disaster to the frogs.

In my next attempt I seem to have acted under the first instinctive impulse which later dominated me — to harness the energies of nature to the service of man. I did this thru the medium of May-bugs — or June-bugs as they are called in America — which were a veritable pest in that country and sometimes broke the branches of trees by the sheer weight of their bodies. The bushes were black with them. I would attach as many as four of them to a crosspiece, rotably arranged on a thin spindle, and transmit the motion of the same to a large disc and so derive considerable "power." These creatures were remarkably efficient, for once they were started they had no sense to stop and continued whirling for hours and hours and the hotter it was the harder they worked. All went well until a strange boy came to the place. He was the son of a retired officer in the Austrian

Army. That urchin ate May-bugs alive and enjoyed them as tho they were the finest blue-point oysters. That disgusting sight terminated my endeavors in this promising field and I have never since been able to touch a May-bug or any other insect for that matter.

After that, I believe, I undertook to take apart and assemble the clocks of my grandfather. In the former operation I was always successful but often failed in the latter. So it came that he brought my work to a sudden halt in a manner not too delicate and it took thirty years before I tackled another clockwork again. Shortly there after I went into the manufacture of a kind of pop-gun which comprised a hollow tube, a piston, and two plugs of hemp. When firing the gun, the piston was prest against the stomach and the tube was pushed back quickly with both hands. The air between the plugs was compressed and raised to high temperature and one of them was expelled with a loud report. The art consisted in selecting a tube of the proper taper from the hollow stalks. I did very well with that gun but my activities interfered with the window panes in our house and met with painful discouragement. If I remember rightly, I then took to carving swords from pieces of furniture which I could conveniently obtain. At that time I was under the sway of the Serbian national poetry and full of admiration for the feats of the heroes. I used to spend hours in mowing down my enemies in the form of corn-stalks which ruined the crops and netted me several spankings from my mother. Moreover these were not of the formal kind but the genuine article.

I had all this and more behind me before I was six years old and had past thru one year of elementary school in the village of Smiljan where I was born. At this juncture we moved to the little city of Gospic nearby. This change of residence was like a calamity to me. It almost broke my heart to part from our pigeons, chickens and sheep, and our magnificent flock of geese which used to rise to the clouds in the morning and return from the feeding grounds at sundown in battle formation, so perfect that it would have put a squadron of the best aviators of the present day to shame. In our new house I was but a prisoner, watching the strange people I saw thru the window blinds. My bashfulness was such that I would rather have faced a roaring lion than one of the city dudes who strolled about. But my hardest trial came on Sunday when I had to dress up and attend the service. There I meet with an accident, the mere thought of which made my blood curdle like sour milk for years afterwards. It was my second adventure in a church. Not long before I was entombed for a night in an old chapel on an inaccessible mountain which was visited only once a year. It was an awful experience, but this one was worse. There was a wealthy lady in town, a good but pompous woman, who used to come to the church gorgeously painted up and attired with an enormous train and attendants. One Sunday I had just finished ringing the bell in the belfry and rushed downstairs when this grand dame was sweeping out and I jumped on her train. It tore off with a ripping noise which sounded like a salvo of musketry fired by raw recruits. My father was livid with rage. He gave me a gentle slap on the cheek, the only corporal punishment he ever administered to me but I almost feel it now. The embarrassment and confusion that followed are indescribable. I was practically ostracised until something else happened which redeemed me in the estimation of the community.

An enterprising young merchant had organized a fire

department. A new fire engine was purchased, uniforms provided and the men drilled for service and parade. The engine was, in reality, a pump to be worked by sixteen men and was beautifully painted red and black. One afternoon the official trial was prepared for and the machine was transported to the river. The entire population turned out to witness the great spectacle. When all the speeches and ceremonies were concluded, the command was given to pump, but not a drop of water came from the nozzle. The professors and experts tried in vain to locate the trouble. The fizzle was complete when I arrived at the scene. My knowledge of the mechanism was nil and I knew next to nothing of air pressure, but instinctively I felt for the suction hose in the water and found that it had collapsed. When I waded in the river and opened it up the water rushed forth and not a few Sunday clothes were spoiled. Archimedes running naked thru the streets of Syracuse and shouting Eureka at the top of his voice did not make a greater impression than myself. I was carried on the shoulders and was the hero of the day.

Upon settling in the city I began a four-years' course in

the so-called Normal School preparatory to my studies at the College or Real Gymnasium. During this period my boyish efforts and exploits, as well as troubles, continued. Among other things I attained the unique distinction of champion crow catcher in the country. My method of procedure was extremely simple. I would go in the forest, hide in the bushes, and imitate the call of the bird. Usually I would get several answers and in a short while a crow would flutter down into the shrubbery near me. After that all I needed to do was to throw a piece of cardboard to distract its attention, jump up and grab it before it could extricate itself from the undergrowth. In this way I would capture as many as I desired. But on one occasion something occurred which made me respect them. I had caught a fine pair of birds and was returning home with a friend. When we left the forest, thousands of crows had gathered making a frightful racket. In a few minutes they rose in pursuit and soon enveloped us. The fun lasted until all of a sudden I received a blow on the back of my head which knocked me down. Then they attacked me viciously. I was compelled to release the two birds and was glad to join my friend who had taken refuge in a cave.

In the schoolroom there were a few mechanical models which interested me and turned my attention to water turbines. I constructed many of these and found great pleasure in operating them. How extraordinary was my life an incident may illustrate. My uncle had no use for this kind of pastime and more than once rebuked me. I was fascinated by a description of Niagara Falls I had perused, and pictured in my imagination a big wheel run by the Falls. I told my uncle that I would go to America and carry out this scheme. Thirty years later I saw my ideas carried out at Niagara and marveled at the unfathomable mystery of the mind.

I made all kinds of other contrivances and contraptions but among these the arbalists I produced were the best. My arrows, when shot, disappeared from sight and at close range traversed a plank of pine one inch thick. Thru the continuous tightening of the bows I developed skin on my stomach very much like that of a crocodile and I am often wondering whether it is due to this exercise that I am able even now to digest cobble-stones! Nor can I pass in silence my performances with the sling which would have enabled me to give a stunning exhibit at the Hippodrome. And now I will tell of one of my feats with this antique implement of war which will strain to the utmost the credulity of the reader. I was practicing while walking with my uncle along the river. The sun was setting, the trout were playful and from time to time one would shoot up into the air, its glistening body sharply defined against a projecting rock beyond. Of course any boy might have hit a fish under these propitious conditions but I undertook a much more difficult task and I foretold to my uncle, to the minutest detail, what I intended doing. I was to hurl a stone to meet the fish, press its body against the rock, and cut it in two. It was no sooner said than done. My uncle looked at me almost scared out of his wits and exclaimed "Vade retro Satanas!" and it was a few days before he spoke to me again. Other records, how ever great, will be eclipsed but I feel that I could peacefully rest on my laurels for a thousand years.

Chapter 3

———◆·✠·◆———

The Discovery of the Rotating
Magnetic Field

At the age of ten I entered the Real Gymnasium which was a new and fairly well equipped institution. In the department of physics were various models of classical scientific apparatus, electrical and mechanical. The demonstrations and experiments performed from time to time by the instructors fascinated me and were undoubtedly a powerful incentive to invention. I was also passionately fond of mathematical studies and often won the professor's praise for rapid calculation. This was due to my acquired facility of visualizing the figures and performing the operations, not in the usual intuitive manner, but as in actual life. Up to a certain degree of complexity it was absolutely the same to me whether I wrote the symbols on the board or conjured them before my mental vision. But freehand drawing, to which many hours of the course were devoted, was an annoyance I could not endure. This was rather remarkable as most of the members of the family excelled in it. Perhaps my aversion was simply due to the predilection I found in undisturbed thought. Had it not been for a few exceptionally stupid boys, who could not do anything at all, my record would have been the worst. It was a serious handicap as under the then existing educational regime, drawing being obligatory, this deficiency threatened to spoil my whole career and my father had considerable trouble in railroading me from one class to another.

In the second year at that institution I became obsessed with the idea of producing continuous motion thru steady air pressure. The pump incident, of which I have told, had set afire my youthful imagination and imprest me with the boundless abilities of a vacuum. I grew frantic in my desire to harness this inexhaustible energy but for a long time I was groping in the dark. Finally, however, my endeavors crystallized in an invention which was to enable me to achieve what no other mortal ever attempted.

Imagine a cylinder freely rotatable on two bearings and partly surrounded by a rectangular trough which fits it perfectly. The open side of the trough is closed by a partition so that the cylindrical segment within the enclosure divides the latter into two compartments entirely separated from each other by air-tight sliding joints. One of these compartments being sealed and once for all exhausted, the other remaining open, a perpetual rotation of the cylinder would result, at least, I thought so. A wooden model was constructed and fitted with infinite care and when I applied the pump on one side and actually observed that there was a tendency to turning, I was delirious with joy. Mechanical flight was the one thing I wanted to accomplish altho still under the discouraging recollection of a bad fall I sustained by jumping with an umbrella from the top of a building. Every day I used to transport myself thru the air to distant regions but could not understand just how I managed to do it. Now I had something concrete—a flying machine with nothing more than a rotating shaft, flapping wings, and—a vacuum of unlimited power! From that time on I made my daily aerial excursions in a vehicle of comfort and luxury as might have befitted King Solomon. It took years before I understood that the atmospheric pressure acted at right angles to the surface of the cylinder and that the slight rotary effort I observed was due to a leak. Tho this knowledge came gradually it gave me a painful shock.

I had hardly completed my course at the Real Gymnasium when I was prostrated with a dangerous illness or rather, a score of them, and my condition became so desperate that I was given up by physicians. During this period I was permitted to read constantly, obtaining books from the Public Library which had been neglected and entrusted to me for classification of the works and preparation of the catalogues. One day I was handed a few volumes of new literature unlike anything I had ever read before and so captivating as to make me utterly forget my hopeless state. They were the earlier works of Mark Twain and to them might have been due the miraculous recovery which followed. Twenty-five years later, when I met Mr. Clemens and we formed a friendship between us, I told him of the experience and was amazed to see that great man of laughter burst into tears.

My studies were continued at the higher Real Gymnasium in Carlstadt, Croatia, where one of my aunts resided. She was a distinguished lady, the wife of a Colonel who was an old war-horse having participated in many battles. I never can forget the three years I past at their home. No fortress in time of war was under a more rigid discipline. I was fed like a canary bird. All the meals were of the highest quality and deliciously prepared but short in quantity by a thousand percent. The slices of ham cut by my aunt were like tissue paper. When the Colonel would put something substantial on my plate she would snatch it away and say excitedly to him: "Be careful, Niko is very delicate." I had a voracious appetite and suffered like Tantalus. But I lived in an atmosphere of refinement and artistic taste quite unusual for those times and conditions. The land was low and marshy and malaria fever never left me while there despite of the enormous amounts of quinin I consumed. Occasionally the river would rise and drive an army of rats into the buildings, devouring everything even to the bundles of the fierce paprika. These pests were to me a welcome diversion. I thinned their ranks by all sorts of means, which won me the unenviable distinction of rat-catcher in the community. At last, however, my course was completed, the misery ended, and I obtained the certificate of maturity which brought me to the cross-roads.

During all those years my parents never wavered in their resolve to make me embrace the clergy, the mere thought of which filled me with dread. I had become intensely interested in electricity under the stimulating influence of my Professor of Physics, who was an ingenious man and often demonstrated the principles by apparatus of his own invention. Among these I recall a device in the shape of a freely rotatable bulb, with tinfoil coatings, which was made to spin rapidly when connected to a static machine. It is impossible for me to convey an adequate idea of the intensity of feeling I experienced in witnessing his exhibitions of these mysterious phenomena. Every impression produced a thousand echoes in my mind. I wanted to know more of this wonderful force; I longed for experiment and investigation and resigned myself to the inevitable with aching heart.

Just as I was making ready for the long journey home I received word that my father wished me to go on a shooting expedition. It was a strange request as he had been always strenuously opposed to this kind of sport. But a few days later I learned that the cholera was raging in that district and, taking advantage of an opportunity, I returned to Gospic in disregard of my parents' wishes. It is incredible how absolutely ignorant people were as to the causes of this scourge which visited the country in intervals of from fifteen to twenty years. They thought that the deadly agents were transmitted thru the air and filled it with pungent odors and smoke. In the meantime they drank the infected water and died in heaps. I contracted the awful disease on the very day of my arrival and altho surviving the crisis, I was confined to bed for nine months with scarcely any ability to move. My energy was completely exhausted and for the second time I found myself at death's door. In one of the sinking spells which was thought to be the last, my father rushed into the room. I still see his pallid face as he tried to cheer me in tones belying his assurance. "Perhaps," I said, "I may get well if you will let me study engineering." "You will go to the best technical institution in the world," he solemnly replied, and I knew that he meant it. A heavy weight was lifted from my mind but the relief would have come too late had it not been for a marvelous cure brought about thru a bitter decoction of a peculiar bean. I came to life like another Lazarus to the utter amazement of everybody.

My father insisted that I spend a year in healthful physical outdoor exercises to which I reluctantly consented. For most of this term I roamed in the mountains, loaded with a hunter's outfit and a bundle of books, and this contact with nature made me stronger in body as well as in mind. I thought and planned, and conceived many ideas almost as a rule delusive. The vision was clear enough but the knowledge of principles was very limited. In one of my inventions I proposed to convey letters and packages across the seas, thru a submarine tube, in spherical containers of sufficient strength to resist the hydraulic pressure. The pumping plant, intended to force the water thru the tube, was accurately figured and designed and all other particulars carefully worked out. Only one trifling detail, of no consequence, was lightly dismist. I assumed an arbitrary velocity of the water and, what is more, took pleasure in making it high, thus arriving at a stupendous performance supported by faultless calculations. Subsequent reflections, however, on the resistance of pipes to fluid flow determined me to make this invention public property.

Another one of my projects was to construct a ring around the equator which would, of course, float freely and could be arrested in its spinning motion by reactionary forces, thus enabling travel at a rate of about one thousand miles an hour, impracticable by rail. The reader will smile. The plan was difficult of execution, I will admit, but not nearly so bad as that of a well-known New York professor, who wanted to pump the air from the torrid to the temperate zones, entirely forgetful of the fact that the Lord had provided a gigantic machine for this very purpose.

Still another scheme, far more important and attractive, was to derive power from the rotational energy of terrestrial bodies. I had discovered that objects on the earth's surface, owing to the diurnal rotation of the globe, are carried by the same alternately in and against the direction of translatory movement. From this results a great change in momentum which could be utilized in the simplest imaginable manner to furnish motive effort in any habitable region of the world. I cannot find words to describe my disappointment when later I realized that I was in the predicament of Archimedes, who vainly sought for a fixt point in the universe.

At the termination of my vacation I was sent to the Polytechnic School in Gratz, Styria, which my father had chosen as one of the oldest and best reputed institutions. That was the moment I had eagerly awaited and I began my studies under good auspices and firmly resolved to succeed. My previous training was above the average, due to my father's teaching and opportunities afforded. I had acquired the knowledge of a number of languages and waded thru the books of several libraries, picking up information more or less useful. Then again, for the first time, I could choose my subjects as I liked, and free-hand drawing was to bother me no more.

I had made up my mind to give my parents a surprise, and during the whole first year I regularly started my work at three o'clock in the morning and continued until eleven at night, no Sundays or holidays excepted. As most of my fellow- students took thinks easily, naturally enough I eclipsed all records. In the course of that year I past thru nine exams and the professors thought I deserved more than the highest qualifications. Armed with their flattering certificates, I went home for a short rest, expecting a triumph, and was mortified when my father made light of these hard won honors. That almost killed my ambition; but later, after he had died, I was pained to find a package of letters which the professors had written him to the effect that unless he took me away from the Institution I would be killed thru overwork.

Thereafter I devoted myself chiefly to physics, mechanics and mathematical studies, spending the hours of leisure in the libraries. I had a veritable rnania for finishing whatever I began, which often got me into difficulties. On one occasion I started to read the works of Voltaire when I learned, to my dismay, that there were close on one hundred large volumes in small print which that monster had written while drinking seventy-two cups of black coffee per diem. It had to be done, but when I laid aside the last book I was very glad, and said, "Never more!"

My first year's showing had won me the appreciation and friendship of several professors. Among these were

Prof. Rogner, who was teaching arithmetical subjects and geometry; Prof. Poeschl, who held the chair of theoretical and experimental physics, and Dr. Alle, who taught integral calculus and specialized in differential equations. This scientist was the most brilliant lecturer to whom I ever listened. He took a special interest in my progress and would frequently remain for an hour or two in the lecture room, giving me problems to solve, in which I delighted. To him I explained a flying machine I had conceived, not an illusionary invention, but one based on sound, scientific principles, which has become realizable thru my turbine and will soon be given to the world. Both Professors Rogner and Poeschl were curious men. The former had peculiar ways of expressing himself and whenever he did so there was a riot, followed by a long and embarrassing pause. Prof. Poeschl was a methodical and thoroly grounded German. He had enormous feet and hands like the paws of a bear, but all of his experiments were skillfully performed with lock-like precision and without a miss.

It was in the second year of my studies that we received a Gramme dynamo from Paris, having the horseshoe form of a laminated field magnet, and a wire-wound armature with a commutator. It was connected up and various effects of the currents were shown. While Prof. Poeschl was making demonstrations, running the machine as a motor, the brushes gave trouble, sparking badly, and I observed that it might be possible to operate a motor without these appliances. But he declared that it could not be done and did me the honor of delivering a lecture on the subject, at the conclusion of which he remarked: "Mr. Tesla may accomplish great things, but he certainly never will do this. It would be equivalent to converting a steadily pulling force, like that of gravity, into a rotary effort. It is a perpetual motion scheme, an impossible idea." But instinct is something which transcends knowledge. We have, undoubtedly, certain finer fibers that enable us to perceive truths when logical deduction, or any other willful effort of the brain, is futile. For a time I wavered, imprest by the professor's authority, but soon became convinced I was right and undertook the task with all the fire and boundless confidence of youth.

I started by first picturing in my mind a direct-current machine, running it and following the changing flow of the currents in the armature. Then I would imagine an alternator and investigate the processes taking place in a similar manner. Next I would visualize systems comprising motors and generators and operate them in various ways. The images I saw were to me perfectly real and tangible. All my remaining term in Gratz was passed in intense but fruitless efforts of this kind, and I almost came to the conclusion that the problem was insolvable.

In 1880 I went to Prague, Bohemia, carrying out my father's wish to complete my education at the University there. It was in that city that I made a decided advance, which consisted in detaching the commutator from the machine and studying the phenomena in this new aspect, but still without result. In the year following there was a sudden change in my views of life. I realized that my parents had been making too great sacrifices on my account and resolved to relieve them of the burden. The wave of the American telephone had just reached the European continent and the system was to be installed in Budapest, Hungary. It appeared an ideal opportunity, all the more as a friend of our family was at the head of the enterprise. It was here that I suffered the complete breakdown of the nerves to which I have referred.

What I experienced during the period of that illness surpasses all belief. My sight and hearing were always extraordinary. I could clearly discern objects in the distance when others saw no trace of them. Several times in my boyhood I saved the houses of our neighbors from fire by hearing the faint crackling sounds which did not disturb their sleep, and calling for help.

In 1899, when I was past forty and carrying on my experiments in Colorado, I could hear very distinctly thunderclaps at a distance of 550 miles. The limit of audition for my young assistants was scarcely more than 150 miles. My ear was thus over thirteen times more sensitive. Yet at that time I was, so to speak, stone deaf in comparison with the acuteness of my hearing while under the nervous strain. In Budapest I could hear the ticking of a watch with three rooms between me and the time-piece. A fly alighting on a table in the room would cause a dull thud in my ear. A carriage passing at a distance of a few miles fairly shook my whole body. The whistle of a locomotive twenty or thirty miles away made the bench or chair on which I sat vibrate so strongly that the pain was unbearable. The ground under my feet trembled continuously. I had to support my bed on rubber cushions to get any rest at all. The roaring noises from near and far often produced the effect of spoken words which would have frightened me had I not been able to resolve them into their accidental components. The sun's rays, when periodically intercepted, would cause blows of such force on my brain that they would stun me. I had to summon all my will power to pass under a bridge or other structure as I experienced a crushing pressure on the skull. In the dark I had the sense of a bat and could detect the presence of an object at a distance of twelve feet by a peculiar creepy sensation on the forehead. My pulse varied from a few to two hundred and sixty beats and all the tissues of the body quivered with twitchings and tremors which was perhaps the hardest to bear. A renowned physician who gave me daily large doses of Bromide of Potassium pronounced my malady unique and incurable.

It is my eternal regret that I was not under the observation of experts in physiology and psychology at that time. I clung desperately to life, but never expected to recover. Can anyone believe that so hopeless a physical wreck could ever be transformed into a man of astonishing strength and tenacity, able to work thirty-eight years almost without a day's interruption, and find himself still strong and fresh in body and mind? Such is my case. A powerful desire to live and to continue the work, and the assistance of a devoted friend and athlete accomplished the wonder. My health returned and with it the vigor of mind. In attacking the problem again I almost regretted that the struggle was soon to end. I had so much energy to spare. When I undertook the task it was not with a resolve such as men often make. With me it was a sacred vow, a question of life and death. I knew that I would perish if I failed. Now I felt that the battle was won. Back in the deep recesses of the brain was the solution, but I could not yet give it outward expression. One afternoon, which is ever present in my recollection, I was enjoying a walk with my friend in the City Park and reciting poetry. At that age I knew entire books by heart, word for word. One of these was Goethe's "Faust." The sun was just setting and reminded me of the glorious passage:

"Sie ruckt und weicht, der Tag ist uberlebt, Dort eilt sie hin und fordert neues Leben.

Oh, dass kein Flugel mich vom Boden hebt Ihr nach und immer nach zu streben!

Ein schoner Traum indessen sie entweicht, Ach, zu des Geistes Flugeln wird so leicht Kein korperlicher Flugel sich gesellen!"

[The glow retreats, done is the day of toil;

It yonder hastes, new fields of life exploring; Ah, that no wing can lift me from the soil Upon its track to follow, follow soaring!

A glorious dream! though now the glories fade.

Alas! the wings that lift the mind no aid

Of wings to lift the body can bequeath me.]

As I uttered these inspiring words the idea came like a flash of lightning and in an instant the truth was revealed. I drew with a stick on the sand the diagrams shown six years later in my address before the American Institute of Electrical Engineers, and my companion understood them perfectly. The images I saw were wonderfully sharp and clear and had the solidity of metal and stone, so much so that I told him: "See my motor here; watch me reverse it." I cannot begin to describe my emotions. Pygmalion seeing his statue come to life could not have been more deeply moved. A thousand secrets of nature which I might have stumbled upon accidentally I would have given for that one which I had wrested from her against all odds and at the peril of my existence.

Chapter 4

———◆◆◆———

The Discovery of the Tesla Coil and Transformer

For a while I gave myself up entirely to the intense enjoyment of picturing machines and devising new forms. It was a mental state of happiness about as complete as I have ever known in life. Ideas came in an uninterrupted stream and the only difficulty I had was to hold them fast. The pieces of apparatus I conceived were to me absolutely real and tangible in every detail, even to the minute marks and signs of wear. I delighted in imagining the motors constantly running, for in this way they presented to mind's eye a more fascinating sight. When natural inclination develops into a passionate desire, one advances towards his goal in seven-league boots. In less than two months I evolved virtually all the types of motors and modifications of the system which are now identified with my name. It was, perhaps, providential that the necessities of existence commanded a temporary halt to this consuming activity of the mind. I came to Budapest prompted by a premature report concerning the telephone enterprise and, as irony of fate willed it, I had to accept a position as draftsman in the Central Telegraph Office of the Hungarian Government at a salary which I deem it my privilege not to disclose! Fortunately, I soon won the interest of the Inspector-in-Chief and was thereafter employed on calculations, designs and estimates in connection with new installations, until the Telephone Exchange was started, when I took charge of the same. The knowledge and practical experience I gained in the course of this work was most valuable and the employment gave me ample opportunities for the exercise of my inventive faculties. I made several improvements in the Central Station apparatus and perfected a telephone repeater or amplifier which was never patented or publicly described but would be creditable to me even today. In recognition of my efficient assistance the organizer of the undertaking, Mr.

Puskas, upon disposing of his business in Budapest, offered me a position in Paris which I gladly accepted.

I never can forget the deep impression that magic city produced on my mind. For several days after my arrival I roamed thru the streets in utter bewilderment of the new spectacle. The attractions were many and irresistible, but, alas, the income was spent as soon as received. When Mr. Puskas asked me how I was getting along in the new sphere, I described the situation accurately in the statement that "the last twenty-nine days of the month are the toughest!" I led a rather strenuous life in what would now be termed "Rooseveltian fashion." Every morning, regardless of weather, I would go from the Boulevard St. Marcel, where I resided, to a bathing house on the Seine, plunge into the water, loop the circuit twenty-seven times and then walk an hour to reach Ivry, where the Company's factory was located. There I would have a woodchopper's breakfast at half-past seven o'clock and then eagerly await the lunch hour, in the meanwhile cracking hard nuts for the Manager of the Works, Mr. Charles Batchellor, who was an intimate friend and assistant of Edison. Here I was thrown in contact with a few Americans who fairly fell in love with me because of my proficiency in billiards. To these men I explained my invention and one of them, Mr. D. Cunningham, Foreman of the Mechanical Department, offered to form a stock company. The proposal seemed to me comical in the extreme. I did not have the faintest conception of what that meant except that it was an American way of doing things. Nothing came of it, however, and during the next few months I had to travel from one to another place in France and Germany to cure the ills of the power plants. On my return to Paris I submitted to one of the administrators of the Company, Mr. Rau, a plan for improving their dynamos and was given an opportunity. My success was complete and the delighted directors accorded me the privilege of developing automatic regulators which were much desired. Shortly after there was some trouble with the lighting plant which had been installed at the new railroad station in Strassburg, Alsace. The wiring was defective and on the occasion of the opening ceremonies a large part of a wall was blown out thru a short-circuit right in the presence of old Emperor William I. The German Government refused to take the plant and the French Company was facing a serious loss. On account of my knowledge of the German language and past experience, I was entrusted with the difficult task of straightening out matters and early in 1883 1 went to Strassburg on that mission.

Some of the incidents in that city have left an indelible record on my memory. By a curious coincidence, a number of men who subsequently achieved fame, lived there about that time. In later life I used to say, "There were bacteria of greatness in that old town. Others caught the disease but I escaped!" The practical work, correspondence, and conferences with officials kept me preoccupied day and night, but, as soon as I was able to manage I undertook the construction of a simple motor in a mechanical shop opposite the railroad station, having brought with me from Paris some material for that purpose. The consummation of the experiment was, however, delayed until the summer of that year when I finally had the satisfaction of seeing rotation effected by alternating currents of different phase, and without sliding contacts or commutator, as I had conceived a year before. It was an exquisite pleasure but not to compare with the delirium of joy following the first revelation.

Among my new friends was the former Mayor of the city, Mr. Bauzin, whom I had already in a measure acquainted with this and other inventions of mine and whose support I endeavored to enlist. He was sincerely devoted to me and put my project before several wealthy persons but, to my mortification, found no response. He wanted to help me in every possible way and the approach of the first of July, 1919, happens to remind me of a form of "assistance" I received from that charming man, which was not financial but none the less appreciated. In 1870, when the Germans invaded the country, Mr. Bauzin had buried a good sized allotment of St. Estephe of 1801 and he came to the conclusion that he knew no worthier person than myself to consume that precious beverage. This, I may say, is one of the unforgettable incidents to which I have referred. My friend urged me to return to Paris as soon as possible and seek support there. This I was anxious to do but my work and negotiations were protracted owing to all sorts of petty obstacles I encountered so that at times the situation seemed hopeless.

Just to give an idea of German thoroness and "efficiency," I may mention here a rather funny experience. An incandescent lamp of 16 c.p. was to be placed in a hallway and upon selecting the proper location I ordered the monteur to run the wires. After working for a while he concluded that the engineer had to be consulted and this was done. The latter made several objections but ultimately agreed that the lamp should be placed two inches from the spot I had assigned, whereupon the work proceeded. Then the engineer became worried and told me that Inspector Averdeck should be notified. That important person called, investigated, debated, and decided that the lamp should be shifted back two inches, which was the place I had marked. It was not long, however, before Averdeck got cold feet himself and advised me that he had informed Ober-Inspector Hieronimus of the matter and that I should await his decision. It was several days before the Ober-Inspector was able to free himself of other pressing duties but at last he arrived and a two-hour debate followed, when he decided to move the lamp two inches farther. My hopes that this was the final act were shattered when the Ober-Inspector returned and said to me: "Regierungsrath Funke is so particular that I would not dare to give an order for placing this lamp without his explicit approval." Accordingly arrangements for a visit from that great man were made. We started cleaning up and polishing early in the morning. Everybody brushed up, I put on my gloves and when Funke came with his retinue he was ceremoniously received. After two hours' deliberation he suddenly exclaimed: "I must be going," and pointing to a place on the ceiling, he ordered me to put the lamp there. It was the exact spot which I had originally chosen.

So it went day after day with variations, but I was determined to achieve at whatever cost and in the end my efforts were rewarded. By the spring of 1884 all the differences were adjusted, the plant formally accepted, and I returned to Paris with pleasing anticipations. One of the administrators had promised me a liberal compensation in case I succeeded, as well as a fair consideration of the improvements I had made in their dynamos and I hoped to realize a substantial sum. There were three administrators whom I shall designate as A,B and C for convenience. When I called on A he told me that B had the say. This gentleman thought that only C could decide and the latter was quite sure that A alone had the power to act. After several laps of this circulus vivios it dawned upon me that my reward was a castle in Spain. The utter failure of my attempts to raise capital for development was another disappointment and when Mr. Batchellor prest me to go to America with a view of redesigning the Edison machines, I determined to try my fortunes in the Land of Golden Promise. But the chance was nearly mist. I liquefied my modest assets, secured accommodations and found myself at the railroad station as the train was pulling out. At that moment I discovered that my money and tickets were gone. What to do was the question. Hercules had plenty of time to deliberate but I had to decide while running alongside the train with opposite feelings surging in my brain like condenser oscillations. Resolve, helped by dexterity, won out in the nick of time and upon passing thru the usual experiences, as trivial as unpleasant, I managed to embark for New York with the remnants of my belongings, some poems and articles I had written, and a package of calculations relating to solutions of an unsolvable integral and to my flying machine. During the voyage I sat most of the time at the stern of the ship watching for an opportunity to save somebody from a watery grave, without the slightest thought of danger. Later when I had absorbed some of the practical American sense I shivered at the recollection and marvelled at my former folly.

I wish that I could put in words my first impressions of this country. In the Arabian Tales I read how genii transported people into a land of dreams to live thru delightful adventures. My case was just the reverse. The genii had carried me from a world of dreams into one of realities. What I had left was beautiful, artistic and fascinating in every way; what I saw here was machined, rough and unattractive. A burly policeman was twirling his stick which looked to me as big as a log. I approached him politely with the request to direct me. "Six blocks down, then to the left," he said, with murder in his eyes. "Is this America?" I asked myself in painful surprise. "It is a century behind Europe in civilization." When I went abroad in 1889 — five years having elapsed since my arrival here — I became convinced that it was more than one hundred years AHEAD of Europe and nothing has happened to this day to change my opinion.

The meeting with Edison was a memorable event in my life. I was amazed at this wonderful man who, without early advantages and scientific training, had accomplished so much. I had studied a dozen languages, delved in literature and art, and had spent my best years in libraries reading all sorts of stuff that fell into my hands, from Newton's "Principia" to the novels of Paul de Kock, and felt that most of my life had been squandered. But it did not take long before I recognized that it was the best thing I could have done. Within a few weeks I had won Edison's confidence and it came about in this way.

The S.S. Oregon, the fastest passenger steamer at that time, had both of its lighting machines disabled and its sailing was delayed. As the superstructure had been built after their installation it was impossible to remove them from the hold. The predicament was a serious one and Edison was much annoyed. In the evening I took the necessary instruments with me and went aboard the vessel where I stayed for the night. The dynamos were in bad condition, having several short-circuits and breaks, but with the assistance of the crew

I succeeded in putting them in good shape. At five o'clock in the morning, when passing along Fifth Avenue on my way to the shop, I met Edison with Batchellor and a few others as they were returning home to retire. "Here is our Parisian running around at night," he said. When I told him that I was coming from the Oregon and had repaired both machines, he looked at me in silence and walked away without another word. But when he had gone some distance I heard him remark: "Batchellor, this is a good man," and from that time on I had full freedom in directing the work. For nearly a year my regular hours were from 10.30 A.M. until 5 o'clock the next morning without a day's exception. Edison said to me: "I have had many hard-working assistants but you take the cake." During this period I designed twenty-four different types of standard machines with short cores and of uniform pattern which replaced the old ones. The Manager had promised me fifty thousand dollars on the completion of this task but it turned out to be a practical joke. This gave me a painful shock and I resigned my position.

Immediately thereafter some people approached me with the proposal of forming an arc light company under my name, to which I agreed. Here finally was an opportunity to develop the motor, but when I broached the subject to my new associates they said: "No, we want the arc lamp. We don't care for this alternating current of yours." In 1886 my system of arc lighting was perfected and adopted for factory and municipal lighting, and I was free, but with no other possession than a beautifully engraved certificate of stock of hypothetical value. Then followed a period of struggle in the new medium for which I was not fitted, but the reward came in the end and in April, 1887, the Tesla Electric Company was organized, providing a laboratory and facilities. The motors I built there were exactly as I had imagined them. I made no attempt to improve the design, but merely reproduced the pictures as they appeared to my vision and the operation was always as I expected.

In the early part of 1888 an arrangement was made with the Westinghouse Company for the manufacture of the motors on a large scale. But great difficulties had still to be overcome. My system was based on the use of low frequency currents and the Westinghouse experts had adopted 133 cycles with the object of securing advantages in the transformation. They did not want to depart from their standard forms of apparatus and my efforts had to be concentrated upon adapting the motor to these conditions. Another necessity was to produce a motor capable of running efficiently at this frequency on two wires which was not easy of accomplishment.

At the close of 1889, however, my services in Pittsburg being no longer essential, I returned to New York and resumed experimental work in a laboratory on Grand Street, where I began immediately the design of high frequency machines. The problems of construction in this unexplored field were novel and quite peculiar and I encountered many difficulties. I rejected the inductor type, fearing that it might not yield perfect sine waves which were so important to resonant action. Had it not been for this I could have saved myself a great deal of labor. Another discouraging feature of the high frequency alternator seemed to be the inconstancy of speed which threatened to impose serious limitations to its use. I had already noted in my demonstrations before the American Institution of Electrical Engineers that several times the tune was lost, necessitating readjustment, and did not yet foresee, what I discovered long afterwards, a means of operating a machine of this kind at a speed constant to such a degree as not to vary more than a small fraction of one revolution between the extremes of load.

From many other considerations it appeared desirable to invent a simpler device for the production of electric oscillations. In 1856 Lord Kelvin had exposed the theory of the condenser discharge, but no practical application of that important knowledge was made. I saw the possibilities and undertook the development of induction apparatus on this principle. My progress was so rapid as to enable me to exhibit at my lecture in 1891 a coil giving sparks of five inches. On that occasion I frankly told the engineers of a defect involved in the transformation by the new method, namely, the loss in the spark gap. Subsequent investigation showed that no matter what medium is employed, be it air, hydrogen, mercury vapor, oil or a stream of electrons, the efficiency is the same. It is a law very much like that governing the conversion of mechanical energy. We may drop a weight from a certain height vertically down or carry it to the lower level along any devious path, it is immaterial insofar as the amount of work is concerned. Fortunately however, this drawback is not fatal as by proper proportioning of the resonant circuits an efficiency of 85 per cent is attainable. Since my early announcement of the invention it has come into universal use and wrought a revolution in many departments. But a still greater future awaits it. When in 1900 I obtained powerful discharges of 100 feet and flashed a current around the globe, I was reminded of the first tiny spark I observed in my Grand Street laboratory and was thrilled by sensations akin to those I felt when I discovered the rotating magnetic field.

Chapter 5

―――◆·⬥·◆―――

The Magnifying Transmitter

As I review the events of my past life I realize how subtle are the influences that shape our destinies. An incident of my youth may serve to illustrate. One winter's day I managed to climb a steep mountain, in company with other boys. The snow was quite deep and a warm southerly wind made it just suitable for our purpose. We amused ourselves by throwing balls which would roll down a certain distance, gathering more or less snow, and we tried to outdo one another in this exciting sport. Suddenly a ball was seen to go beyond the limit, swelling to enormous proportions until it became as big as a house and plunged thundering into the valley below with a force that made the ground tremble. I looked on spellbound, incapable of understanding what had happened. For weeks afterward the picture of the avalanche was before my eyes and I wondered how anything so small could grow to such an immense size. Ever since that time the magnification of feeble actions fascinated me, and when, years later, I took up the experimental study of mechanical and electrical resonance, I was keenly interested from the very start. Possibly, had it not been for that early powerful impression, I might not have followed up the little spark I obtained with my coil and never developed my best invention, the true history of which I'll tell here for the first time.

"Lionhunters" have often asked me which of my discoveries I prize most. This depends on the point of view. Not a few technical men, very able in their special departments, but dominated by a pedantic spirit and nearsighted, have asserted that excepting the induction motor I have given to the world little of practical use. This is a grievous mistake. A new idea must not be judged by its immediate results. My alternating system of power transmission came at a psychological moment, as a long-sought answer to pressing industrial questions, and altho considerable resistance had to be overcome and opposing interests reconciled, as usual, the commercial introduction could not be long delayed. Now, compare this situation with that confronting my turbine, for example. One should think that so simple and beautiful an invention, possessing many features of an ideal motor, should be adopted at once and, undoubtedly, it would under similar conditions. But the prospective effect of the rotating field was not to render worthless existing machinery; on the contrary, it was to give it additional value. The system lent itself to new enterprise as well as to improvement of the old. My turbine is an advance of a character entirely different. It is a radical departure in the sense that its success would mean the abandonment of the antiquated types of prime movers on which billions of dollars have been spent. Under such circumstances the progress must needs be slow and perhaps the greatest impediment is encountered in the prejudicial opinions created in the minds of experts by organized opposition.

Only the other day I had a disheartening experience when I met my friend and former assistant, Charles F. Scott, now professor of Electrical Engineering at Yale. I had not seen him for a long time and was glad to have an opportunity for a little chat at my office. Our conversation naturally enough drifted on my turbine and I became heated to a high degree. "Scott," I exclaimed, carried away by the vision of a glorious future, "my turbine will scrap all the heat-engines in the world." Scott stroked his chin and looked away thoughtfully, as though making a mental calculation. "That will make quite a pile of scrap," he said, and left without another word!

These and other inventions of mine, however, were nothing more than steps forward in certain directions. In evolving them I simply followed the inborn sense to improve the present devices without any special thought of our far more imperative necessities. The "Magnifying Transmitter" was the product of labors extending through years, having for their chief object the solution of problems which are infinitely more important to mankind than mere industrial development.

If my memory serves me right, it was in November, 1890, that I performed a laboratory experiment which was one of the most extraordinary and spectacular ever recorded in the annals of science. In investigating the behaviour of high frequency currents I had satisfied myself that an electric field of sufficient intensity could be produced in a room to light up electrodeless vacuum tubes. Accordingly, a transformer was built to test the theory and the first trial proved a marvelous success. It is difficult to appreciate what those strange phenomena meant at that time. We crave for new sensations but soon become indifferent to them. The wonders of yesterday are today common occurrences. When my tubes were first publicly exhibited they were viewed with amazement impossible to describe. From all parts of the world I received urgent invitations and numerous honors and other flattering inducements were offered to me, which I declined.

But in 1892 the demands became irresistible and I went to London where I delivered a lecture before the Institution of Electrical Engineers. It had been my intention to leave immediately for Paris in compliance with a similar obligation, but Sir James Dewar insisted on my appearing before the Royal Institution. I was a man of firm resolve but succumbed easily to the forceful arguments of the great Scotsman. He pushed me into a chair and poured out half a glass of a wonderful brown fluid which sparkled in all sorts of iridescent colors and tasted like nectar. "Now," said he. "you are sitting in Faraday's chair and you are enjoying whiskey he used to drink." In both aspects it was an enviable experience. The next evening I gave a demonstration before that Institution, at the termination of which Lord Rayleigh addressed the audience and his generous words gave me the first start in these endeavors. I fled from London and later from Paris to escape favors showered upon me, and journeyed to my home where I passed through a most painful ordeal and illness. Upon regaining my health I began to formulate plans for the resumption of work in America. Up to that time I never realized that I possessed any particular gift of discovery but Lord Rayleigh, whom I always considered as an ideal man of science, had said so and if that was the case I felt that I should concentrate on some big idea.

One day, as I was roaming in the mountains, I sought shelter from an approaching storm. The sky became overhung with heavy clouds but somehow the rain was delayed until, all of a sudden, there was a lightning flash and a few moments after a deluge. This observation set me thinking. It was manifest that the two phenomena were closely related, as cause and effect, and a little reflection led me to the conclusion that the electrical energy involved in the precipitation of the water was inconsiderable, the function of lightning being much like that of a sensitive trigger.

Here was a stupendous possibility of achievement. If we could produce electric effects of the required quality, this whole planet and the conditions of existence on it could be transformed. The sun raises the water of the oceans and winds drive it to distant regions where it remains in a state of most delicate balance. If it were in our power to upset it when and wherever desired, this mighty life- sustaining stream could be at will controlled. We could irrigate arid deserts, create lakes and rivers and provide motive power in unlimited amounts. This would be the most efficient way of harnessing the sun to the uses of man. The consummation depended on our ability to develop electric forces of the order of those in nature. It seemed a hopeless undertaking, but I made up my mind to try it and immediately on my return to the United States, in the Summer of 1892, work was begun which was to me all the more attractive, because a means of the same kind was necessary for the successful transmission of energy without wires.

The first gratifying result was obtained in the spring of the succeeding year when I reached tensions of about 1,000,000 volts with my conical coil. That was not much in the light of the present art, but it was then considered a feat. Steady progress was made until the destruction of my laboratory by fire in 1895, as may be judged from an article by T. C. Martin which appeared in the April number of the Century Magazine. This calamity set me back in many ways and most of that year had to be devoted to planning and reconstruction. However, as soon as circumstances permitted, I returned to the task.

Although I knew that higher electro-motive forces were attainable with apparatus of larger dimensions, I had an instinctive perception that the object could be accomplished by the proper design of a comparatively small and compact transformer. In carrying on tests with a secondary in the form of a flat spiral, as illustrated in my patents, the absence of streamers surprised me, and it was not long before I discovered that this was due to the position of the turns and their mutual action. Profiting from this observation I resorted to the use of a high tension conductor with turns of considerable diameter sufficiently separated to keep down the distributed capacity, while at the same time preventing undue accumulation of the charge at any point. The application of this principle enabled me to produce pressures of 4,000,000 volts, which was about the limit obtainable in my new laboratory at Houston Street, as the discharges extended through a distance of 16 feet. A photograph of this transmitter was published in the Electrical Review of November, 1898.

In order to advance further along this line I had to go into the open, and in the spring of 1899, having completed preparations for the erection of a wireless plant, I went to Colorado where I remained for more than one year. Here I introduced other improvements and refinements which made it possible to generate currents of any tension that may be desired. Those who are interested will find some information in regard to the experiments I conducted there in my article, "The Problem of Increasing Human Energy" in the Century

Magazine of June, 1900, to which I have referred on a previous occasion.

I have been asked by the ELECTRICAL EXPERIMENTER to be quite explicit on this subject so that my young friends among the readers of the magazine will clearly understand the construction and operation of my "Magnifying Transmitter" and the purposes for which it is intended. Well, then, in the first place, it is a resonant transformer with a secondary in which the parts, charged to a high potential, are of considerable area and arranged in space along ideal enveloping surfaces of very large radii of curvature, and at proper distances from one another thereby insuring a small electric surface density everywhere so that no leak can occur even if the conductor is bare. It is suitable for any frequency, from a few to many thousands of cycles per second, and can be used in the production of currents of tremendous volume and moderate pressure, or of smaller amperage and immense electromotive force. The maximum electric tension is merely dependent on the curvature of the surfaces on which the charged elements are situated and the area of the latter.

Judging from my past experience, as much as 100,000,000

volts are perfectly practicable. On the other hand currents of many thousands of amperes may be obtained in the antenna. A plant of but very moderate dimensions is required for such performances. Theoretically, a terminal of less than 90 feet in diameter is sufficient to develop an electromotive force of that magnitude while for antenna currents of from 2,000-4,000 amperes at the usual frequencies it need not be larger than 30 feet in diameter.

In a more restricted meaning this wireless transmitter is one in which the Hertz-wave radiation is an entirely negligible quantity as compared with the whole energy, under which condition the damping factor is extremely small and an enormous charge is stored in the elevated capacity. Such a circuit may then be excited with impulses of any kind, even of low frequency and it will yield sinusoidal and continuous oscillations like those of an alternator.

Taken in the narrowest significance of the term, however, it is a resonant transformer which, besides possessing these qualities, is accurately proportioned to fit the globe and its electrical constants and properties, by virtue of which design it becomes highly efficient and effective in the wireless transmission of energy. Distance is then absolutely eliminated, there being no diminution in the intensity of the transmitted impulses. It is even possible to make the actions increase with the distance from the plant according to an exact mathematical law.

This invention was one of a number comprised in my "World-System" of wireless transmission which I undertook to commercialize on my return to New York in 1900. As to the immediate purposes of my enterprise, they were clearly outlined in a technical statement of that period from which I quote:

"The 'World-System' has resulted from a combination of several original discoveries made by the inventor in the course of long continued research and experimentation. It makes possible not only the instantaneous and precise wireless transmission of any kind of signals, messages or characters, to all parts of the world, but also the inter-connection of the existing telegraph, telephone, and other signal stations without any change in their present equipment. By its means, for instance, a telephone subscriber here may call up and talk to any other subscriber on the Globe. An inexpensive receiver, not bigger than a watch, will enable him to listen anywhere, on land or sea, to a speech delivered or music played in some other place, however distant. These examples are cited merely to give an idea of the possibilities of this great scientific advance, which annihilates distance and makes that perfect natural conductor, the Earth, available for all the innumerable purposes which human ingenuity has found for a line-wire. One far-reaching result of this is that any device capable of being operated thru one or more wires (at a distance obviously restricted) can likewise be actuated, without artificial conductors and with the same facility and accuracy, at distances to which there are no limits other than those imposed by the physical dimensions of the Globe. Thus, not only will entirely new fields for commercial exploitation be opened up by this ideal method of transmission but the old ones vastly extended.

The 'World-System' is based on the application of the following important inventions and discoveries:

1.The 'Tesla Transformer.' This apparatus is in the production of electrical vibrations as revolutionary as gunpowder was in warfare. Currents many times stronger than any ever generated in the usual ways, and sparks over one hundred feet long, have been produced by the inventor with an instrument of this kind.

2.The 'Magnifying Transmitter.' This is Tesla's best invention, a peculiar transformer specially adapted to excite the Earth, which is in the transmission of electrical energy what the telescope is in astronomical observation. By the use of this marvelous device he has already set up electrical movements of greater intensity than those of lightning and passed a current, sufficient to light more than two hundred incandescent lamps, around the Globe.

3.The 'Tesla Wireless System.' This system comprises a number of improvements and is the only means known for transmitting economically electrical energy to a distance without wires. Careful tests and measurements in connection with an experimental station of great activity, erected by the inventor in Colorado, have demonstrated that power in any desired amount can be conveyed, clear across the Globe if necessary, with a loss not exceeding a few per cent.

4.The 'Art of Individualization.' This invention of Tesla's is to primitive 'tuning' what refined language is to unarticulated expression. It makes possible the transmission of signals or messages absolutely secret and exclusive both in the active and passive aspect, that is, non-interfering as well as non-interferable. Each signal is like an individual of unmistakable identity and there is virtually no limit to the number of stations or instruments which can be simultaneously operated without the slightest mutual disturbance.

5. 'The Terrestrial Stationary Waves.' This wonderful discovery, popularly explained, means that the Earth is responsive to electrical vibrations of definite pitch just as a tuning fork to certain waves of sound. These particular electrical vibrations, capable of powerfully exciting the Globe, lend themselves to innumerable uses of great importance commercially and in many other respects.

The first 'World-System' power plant can be put in operation in nine months. With this power plant it will be practicable to attain electrical activities up to ten million horsepower and it is designed to serve for as many technical achievements as are possible without due expense. Among these the following may be mentioned:

(1) The inter-connection of the existing telegraph exchanges or offices all over the world;

(2) The establishment of a secret and non-interferable government telegraph service;

(3) The inter-connection of all the present telephone exchanges or offices on the Globe;

(4) The universal distribution of general news, by telegraph or telephone, in connection with the Press;

(5) The establishment of such a 'World-System' of intelligence transmission for exclusive private use;

(6) The inter-connection and operation of all stock tickers of the world;

(7) The establishment of a 'World-System' of musical distribution, etc.;

(8) The universal registration of time by cheap clocks indicating the hour with astronomical precision and requiring no attention whatever;

(9) The world transmission of typed or handwritten characters, letters, checks, etc.;

(10) The establishment of a universal marine service enabling the navigators of all ships to steer perfectly without

compass, to determine the exact location, hour and speed, to prevent collisions and disasters, etc.;

(11) The inauguration of a system of world-printing on land and sea;

(12) The world reproduction of photographic pictures and all kinds of drawings or records."

I also proposed to make demonstrations in the wireless transmission of power on a small scale but sufficient to carry conviction. Besides these I referred to other and incomparably more important applications of my discoveries which will be disclosed at some future date.

A plant was built on Long Island with a tower 187 feet high, having a spherical terminal about 68 feet in diameter. These dimensions were adequate for the transmission of virtually any amount of energy. Originally only from 200 to 300 K.W. were provided but I intended to employ later several thousand horsepower. The transmitter was to emit a wave complex of special characteristics and I had devised a unique method of telephonic control of any amount of energy.

The tower was destroyed two years ago but my projects are being developed and another one, improved in some features, will be constructed. On this occasion I would contradict the widely circulated report that the structure was demolished by the Government which owing to war conditions, might have created prejudice in the minds of those who may not know that the papers, which thirty years ago conferred upon me the honor of American citizenship, are always kept in a safe, while my orders, diplomas, degrees, gold medals and other distinctions are packed away in old trunks. If this report had a foundation I would have been refunded a large sum of money which I expended in the construction of the tower. On the contrary it was in the interest of the Government to preserve it, particularly as it would have made possible—to mention just one valuable result—the location of a submarine in any part of the world. My plant, services, and all my improvements have always been at the disposal of the officials and ever since the outbreak of the European conflict I have been working at a sacrifice on several inventions of mine relating to aerial navigation, ship propulsion and wireless transmission which are of the greatest importance to the country. Those who are well informed know that my ideas have revolutionized the industries of the United States and I am not aware that there lives an inventor who has been, in this respect, as fortunate as myself especially as regards the use of his improvements in the war. I have refrained from publicly expressing myself on this subject before as it seemed improper to dwell on personal matters while all the world was in dire trouble.

I would add further, in view of various rumors which have reached me, that Mr. J. Pierpont Morgan did not interest himself with me in a business way but in the same large spirit in which he has assisted many other pioneers. He carried out his generous promise to the letter and it would have been most unreasonable to expect from him anything more. He had the highest regard for my attainments and gave me every evidence of his complete faith in my ability to ultimately achieve what I had set out to do. I am unwilling to accord to some smallminded and jealous individuals the satisfaction of having thwarted my efforts. These men are to me nothing more than microbes of a nasty disease. My project was retarded by laws of nature. The world was not prepared for it. It was too far ahead of time. But the same laws will prevail in the end and make it a triumphal success.

Chapter 6

——❖·✿·❖——

The Art of Telautomatics

No subject to which I have ever devoted myself has called for such concentration of mind and strained to so dangerous a degree the finest fibers of my brain as the system of which the Magnifying Transmitter is the foundation. I put all the intensity and vigor of youth in the development of the rotating field discoveries, but those early labors were of a different character. Although strenuous in the extreme, they did not involve that keen and exhausting discernment which had to be exercised in attacking the many puzzling problems of the wireless. Despite my rare physical endurance at that period the abused nerves finally rebelled and I suffered a complete collapse, just as the consummation of the long and difficult task was almost in sight.

Without doubt I would have paid a greater penalty later, and very likely my career would have been prematurely terminated, had not providence equipt me with a safety device, which has seemed to improve with advancing years and unfailingly comes into play when my forces are at an end. So long as it operates I am safe from danger, due to overwork, which threatens other inventors and, incidentally, I need no vacations which are indispensable to most people. When I am all but used up I simply do as the darkies, who "naturally fall asleep while white folks worry." To venture a theory out of my sphere, the body probably accumulates little by little a definite quantity of some toxic agent and I sink into a nearly lethargic state which lasts half an hour to the minute. Upon awakening I have the sensation as though the events immediately preceding had occurred very long ago, and if I attempt to continue the interrupted train of thought I feel a veritable mental nausea. Involuntarily I then turn to other work and am surprised at the freshness of the mind and ease with which I overcome obstacles that had baffled me before. After weeks or months my passion for the temporarily abandoned invention returns and I invariably find answers to all the vexing questions with scarcely any effort.

In this connection I will tell of an extraordinary experience which may be of interest to students of psychology. I had produced a striking phenomenon with my grounded transmitter and was endeavoring to ascertain its true significance in relation to the currents propagated through the earth. It seemed a hopeless undertaking, and for more than a year I worked unremittingly, but in vain. This profound study so entirely absorbed me that I became forgetful of everything else, even of my undermined health. At last, as I was at the point of breaking down, nature applied the preservative inducing lethal sleep. Regaining my senses I realized with consternation that I was unable to visualize scenes from my life except those of infancy, the very first ones that had entered my consciousness. Curiously enough, these appeared before my vision with startling distinctness and afforded me welcome relief. Night after night, when retiring, I would think of them and more and more of my previous existence was revealed. The image of my mother was always the principal figure in the spectacle that slowly unfolded, and a consuming desire to see her again gradually took possession of me. This feeling grew so strong that I resolved to drop all work and satisfy my longing. But I found it too hard to break away from the laboratory, and several months elapsed during which I had succeeded in reviving all the impressions of my past life up to the spring of 1892. In the next picture that came out of the mist of oblivion, I saw myself at the Hotel de la Paix in Paris just coming to from one of my peculiar sleeping spells, which had been caused by prolonged exertion of the brain. Imagine the pain and distress I felt when it flashed upon my mind that a dispatch was handed to me at that very moment bearing the sad news that my mother was dying. I remembered how I made the long journey home without an hour of rest and how she passed away after weeks of agony! It was especially remarkable that during all this period of partially obliterated memory I was fully alive to everything touching on the subject of my research. I could recall the smallest details and the least significant observations in my experiments and even recite pages of text and complex mathematical formulae.

My belief is firm in a law of compensation. The true rewards are ever in proportion to the labor and sacrifices made. This is one of the reasons why I feel certain that of all my inventions, the Magnifying Transmitter will prove most important and valuable to future generations. I am prompted to this prediction not so much by thoughts of the commercial and industrial revolution which it will surely bring about, but of the humanitarian consequences of the many achievements it makes possible. Considerations of mere utility weigh little in the balance against the higher benefits of civilization. We are confronted with portentous problems which can not be solved just by providing for our material existence, however abundantly. On the contrary, progress in this direction is fraught with hazards and perils not less menacing than those born from want and suffering. If we were to release the energy of atoms or discover some other way of developing cheap and unlimited power at any point of the globe this accomplishment, instead of being a blessing, might bring disaster to mankind in giving rise to dissension and anarchy which would ultimately result in the enthronement of the hated regime of force. The greatest good will comes from technical improvements tending to unification and harmony, and my wireless transmitter is preeminently such. By its means the human voice and likeness will be reproduced everywhere and factories driven thousands of miles from waterfalls furnishing the power; aerial machines will be propelled around the earth without a stop and the sun's energy controlled to create lakes and rivers for motive purposes and transformation of arid deserts into fertile land. Its introduction for telegraphic, telephonic and similar uses will automatically cut out the statics and all other interferences which at present impose narrow limits to the application of the wireless.

This is a timely topic on which a few words might not be amiss.

During the past decade a number of people have arrogantly claimed that they had succeeded in doing away with this impediment. I have carefully examined all of the arrangements described and tested most of them long before they were publicly disclosed, but the finding was uniformly negative. A recent official statement from the U.S. Navy may, perhaps, have taught some beguilable news editors how to appraise these announcments at their real worth. As a rule the attempts are based on theories so fallacious that whenever they come to my notice I can not help thinking in a lighter vein. Quite recently a new discovery was heralded, with a deafening flourish of trumpets, but it proved another case of a mountain bringing forth a mouse.

This reminds me of an exciting incident which took place years ago when I was conducting my experiments with currents of high frequency. Steve Brodie had just jumped off the Brooklyn Bridge. The feat has been vulgarized since by imitators, but the first report electrified New York. I was very impressionable then and frequently spoke of the daring printer. On a hot afternoon I felt the necessity of refreshing myself and stepped into one of the popular thirty thousand institutions of this great city where a delicious twelve per-cent beverage was served which can now be had only by making a trip to the poor and devastated countries of Europe. The attendance was large and not overdistinguished and a matter was discussed which gave me an admirable opening for the careless remark: "This is what I said when I jumped off the bridge." No sooner had I uttered these words than I felt like the companion of Timotheus in the poem of Schiller. In an instant there was a pandemonium and a dozen voices cried: "It is Brodie!" I threw a quarter on the counter and bolted for the door but the crowd was at my heels with yells: "Stop, Steve!" which must have been misunderstood for many persons tried to hold me up as I ran frantically for my haven of refuge. By darting around corners I fortunately managed — through the medium of a fire-escape — to reach the laboratory where I threw off my coat, camouflaged myself as a hard-working blacksmith, and started the forge. But these precautions proved unnecessary; I had eluded my pursuers. For many years afterward, at night, when imagination turns into spectres the trifling troubles of the day, I often thought, as I tossed on the bed, what my fate would have been had that mob caught me and found out that I was not Steve Brodie!

Now the engineer, who lately gave an account before a technical body of a novel remedy against statics based on a "heretofore unknown law of nature," seems to have been as reckless as myself when he contended that these disturbances propagate up and down, while those of a transmitter proceed along the earth. It would mean that a condenser, as this globe, with its gaseous envelope, could be charged and discharged in a manner quite contrary to the fundamental teachings propounded in every elemental text-book of physics. Such a supposition would have been condemned as erroneous, even in Franklin's time, for the facts bearing on this were then well known and the identity between atmospheric electricity and that developed by machines was fully established. Obviously, natural and artificial disturbances propagate through the earth and the air in exactly the same way, and both set up electromotive forces in the horizontal, as well as vertical, sense. Interference can not be overcome by any such methods as were proposed. The truth is this: in the air the potential increases at the rate of about fifty volts per foot of elevation, owing to which there may be a difference of pressure amounting to twenty, or even forty thousand volts between the upper and lower ends of the antenna. The masses of the charged atmosphere are constantly in motion and give up electricity to the conductor, not continuously but rather disruptively, this producing a grinding noise in a sensitive telephonic receiver. The higher the terminal and the greater the space encompassed by the wires, the more pronounced is the effect, but it must be understood that it is purely local and has little to do with the real trouble.

In 1900, while perfecting my wireless system, one form of apparatus comprised four antennae. These were carefully calibrated to the same frequency and connected in multiple with the object of magnifying the action, in receiving from any direction. When I desired to ascertain the origin of the transmitted impulses, each diagonally situated pair was put in series with a primary coil energizing the detector circuit. In the former case the sound was loud in the telephone; in the latter it ceased, as expected, the two antennae neutralizing each other, but the true statics manifested themselves in both instances and I had to devise special preventives embodying different principles.

By employing receivers connected to two points of the ground, as suggested by me long ago, this trouble caused by the charged air, which is very serious in the structures as now built, is nullified and besides, the liability of all kinds of interference is reduced to about one-half, because of the directional character of the circuit. This was perfectly self-evident, but came as a revelation to some simple-minded wireless folks whose experience was confined to forms of apparatus that could have been improved with an axe, and they have been disposing of the bear's skin before killing him. If it were true that strays performed such antics, it would be easy to get rid of them by receiving without aerials. But, as a matter of fact, a wire buried in the ground which, conforming to this view, should be absolutely immune, is more susceptible to certain extraneous impulses than one placed vertically in the air. To state it fairly, a slight progress has been made, but not by virtue of any particular method or device. It was achieved simply by discarding the enormous structures, which are bad enough for transmission but wholly unsuitable for reception, and adopting a more appropriate type of receiver. As I pointed out in a previous article, to dispose of this difficulty for good, a radical change must be made in the system, and the sooner this is done the better.

It would be calamitous, indeed, if at this time when the art is in its infancy and the vast majority, not excepting even experts, have no conception of its ultimate possibilities, a measure would be rushed through the legislature making it a government monopoly. This was proposed a few weeks ago by Secretary Daniels, and no doubt that distinguished official has made his appeal to the Senate and House of Representatives with sincere conviction. But universal evidence unmistakably shows that the best results are always obtained in healthful commercial competition. There are, however, exceptional reasons why wireless should be given the fullest freedom of development. In the first place it offers prospects immeasurably greater and more vital to betterment of human life than any other invention or discovery in the history of man. Then again, it must be understood that this wonderful art has been, in its entirety, evolved here and can be called "American" with more right and propriety than the telephone, the incandescent lamp or the aeroplane. Enterprising press agents and stock jobbers have been so successful in spreading misinformation that even so excellent a periodical as the Scientific American accords the chief credit to a foreign country. The Germans, of course, gave us the Hertz-waves and the Russian, English,

French and Italian experts were quick in using them for signaling purposes. It was an obvious application of the new agent and accomplished with the old classical and unimproved induction coil—scarcely anything more than another kind of heliography. The radius of transmission was very limited, the results attained of little value, and the Hertz oscillations, as a means for conveying intelligence, could have been advantageously replaced by sound-waves, which I advocated in 1891. Moreover, all of these attempts were made three years after the basic principles of the wireless system, which is universally employed to-day, and its potent instrumentalities had been clearly described and developed in America. No trace of those Hertzian appliances and methods remains today. We have proceeded in the very opposite direction and what has been done is the product of the brains and efforts of citizens of this country. The fundamental patents have expired and the opportunities are open to all. The chief argument of the Secretary is based on interference. According to his statement, reported in the New York Herald of July 29th, signals from a powerful station can be intercepted in every village of the world . In view of this fact, which was demonstrated in my experiments of 1900, it would be of little use to impose restrictions in the United States.

As throwing light on this point, I may mention that only recently an odd looking gentleman called on me with the object of enlisting my services in the construction of world transmitters in some distant land. "We have no money," he said, "but carloads of solid gold and we will give you a liberal amount." I told him that I wanted to see first what will be done with my inventions in America, and this ended the interview. But I am satisfied that some dark forces are at work, and as time goes on the maintenance of continuous communication will be rendered more difficult. The only remedy is a system immune against interruption. It has been perfected, it exists, and all that is necessary is to put it in operation.

The terrible conflict is still uppermost in the minds and perhaps the greatest importance will be attached to the Magnifying Transmitter as a machine for attack and defense, more particularly in connection with Telautomatics. This invention is a logical outcome of observations begun in my boyhood and continued thruout my life. When the first results were published the Electrical Review stated editorially that it would become one of the "most potent factors in the advance and civilization of mankind." The time is not distant when this prediction will be fulfilled. In 1898 and 1900 it was offered to the Government and might have been adopted were I one of those who would go to Alexander's shepherd when they want a favor from Alexander. At that time I really thought that it would abolish war, because of its unlimited destructiveness and exclusion of the personal element of combat. But while I have not lost faith in its potentialities, my views have changed since.

War can not be avoided until the physical cause for its recurrence is removed and this, in the last analysis, is the vast extent of the planet on which we live. Only thru annihilation of distance in every respect, as the conveyance of intelligence, transport of passengers and supplies and transmission of energy will conditions be brought about some day, insuring permanency of friendly relations. What we now want most is closer contact and better understanding between individuals and communities all over the earth, and the elimination of that fanatic devotion to exalted ideals of national egoism and pride which is always prone to plunge the world into primeval barbarism and strife. No league or parliamentary act of any kind will ever prevent such a calamity. These are only new devices for putting the weak at the mercy of the strong. I have expressed myself in this regard fourteen years ago, when a combination of a few leading governments — a sort of Holy Alliance — was advocated by the late Andrew Carnegie, who may be fairly considered as the father of this idea, having given to it more publicity and impetus than anybody else prior to the efforts of the President. While it can not be denied that such a pact might be of material advantage to some less fortunate peoples, it can not attain the chief object sought. Peace can only come as a natural consequence of universal enlightenment and merging of races, and we are still far from this blissful realization.

As I view the world of today, in the light of the gigantic struggle we have witnessed, I am filled with conviction that the interests of humanity would be best served if the United States remained true to its traditions and kept out of "entangling alliances." Situated as it is, geographically, remote from the theaters of impending conflicts, without incentive to territorial aggrandizement, with inexhaustible resources and immense population thoroly imbued with the spirit of liberty and right, this country is placed in a unique and privileged position. It is thus able to exert, independently, its colossal strength and moral force to the benefit of all, more judiciously and effectively, than as member of a league.

In one of these biographical sketches, published in the ELECTRICAL EXPERIMENTER, I have dwelt on the circumstances of my early life and told of an affliction which compelled me to unremitting exercise of imagination and self observation. This mental activity, at first involuntary under the pressure of illness and suffering, gradually became second nature and led me finally to recognize that I was but an automaton devoid of free will in thought and action and merely responsive to the forces of the environment. Our bodies are of such complexity of structure, the motions we perform are so numerous and involved, and the external impressions on our sense organs to such a degree delicate and elusive that it is hard for the average person to grasp this fact. And yet nothing is more convincing to the trained investigator than the mechanistic theory of life which had been, in a measure, understood and propounded by Descartes three hundred years ago. But in his time many important functions of our organism were unknown and, especially with respect to the nature of light and the construction and operation of the eye, philosophers were in the dark.

In recent years the progress of scientific research in these fields has been such as to leave no room for a doubt in regard to this view on which many works have been published. One of its ablest and most eloquent exponents is, perhaps, Felix Le Dantec, formerly assistant of Pasteur. Prof. Jacques Loeb has performed remarkable experiments in heliotropism, clearly establishing the controlling power of light in lower forms of organisms, and his latest book, "Forced Movements," is revelatory. But while men of science accept this theory simply as any other that is recognized, to me it is a truth which I hourly demonstrate by every act and thought of mine. The consciousness of the external impression prompting me to any kind of exertion, physical or mental, is ever present in my mind. Only on very rare occasions, when I was in a state of exceptional concentration, have I found difficulty in locating the original impulses.

The by far greater number of human beings are never aware of what is passing around and within them, and millions fall victims of disease and die prematurely just on this account. The commonest everyday occurrences appear to them mysterious and inexplicable. One may feel a sudden wave of sadness and rake his brain for an explanation when he might have noticed that it was caused by a cloud cutting off the rays of the sun. He may see the image of a friend dear to him under conditions which he construes as very peculiar, when only shortly before he has passed him in the street or seen his photograph somewhere. When he loses a collar button he fusses and swears for an hour, being unable to visualize his previous actions and locate the object directly. Deficient observation is merely a form of ignorance and responsible for the many morbid notions and foolish ideas prevailing. There is not more than one out of every ten persons who does not believe in telepathy and other psychic manifestations, spiritualism and communion with the dead, and who would refuse to listen to willing or unwilling deceivers.

Just to illustrate how deeply rooted this tendency has become even among the clearheaded American population, I may mention a comical incident.

Shortly before the war, when the exhibition of my turbines in this city elicited widespread comment in the technical papers, I anticipated that there would be a scramble among manufacturers to get hold of the invention, and I had particular designs on that man from Detroit who has an uncanny faculty for accumulating millions. So confident was I that he would turn up some day, that I declared this as certain to my secretary and assistants. Sure enough, one fine morning a body of engineers from the Ford Motor Company presented themselves with the request of discussing with me an important project. "Didn't I tell you?" I remarked triumphantly to my employees, and one of them said, "You are amazing, Mr. Tesla; everything comes out exactly as you predict." As soon as these hard-headed men were seated I, of course, immediately began to extol the wonderful features of my turbine, when the spokesmen interrupted me and said,

"We know all about this, but we are on a special errand. We have formed a psychological society for the investigation of psychic phenomena and we want you to join us in this undertaking." I suppose those engineers never knew how near they came to being fired out of my office.

Ever since I was told by some of the greatest men of the time, leaders in science whose names are immortal, that I am possessed of an unusual mind, I bent all my thinking faculties on the solution of great problems regardless of sacrifice. For many years I endeavored to solve the enigma of death, and watched eagerly for every kind of spiritual indication. But only once in the course of my existence have I had an experience which momentarily impressed me as supernatural. It was at the time of my mother's death. I had become completely exhausted by pain and long vigilance, and one night was carried to a building about two blocks from our home. As I lay helpless there, I thought that if my mother died while I was away from her bedside she would surely give me a sign. Two or three months before I was in London in company with my late friend, Sir William Crookes, when spiritualism was discussed, and I was under the full sway of these thoughts. I might not have paid attention to other men, but was susceptible to his arguments as it was his epochal work on radiant matter, which I had read as a student, that made me embrace the electrical career. I reflected that the conditions for a look into the beyond were most favorable, for my mother was a woman of genius and particularly excelling in the powers of intuition. During the whole night every fiber in my brain was strained in expectancy, but nothing happened until early in the morning, when I fell in a sleep, or perhaps a swoon, and saw a cloud carrying angelic figures of marvelous beauty, one of whom gazed upon me lovingly and gradually assumed the features of my mother. The appearance slowly floated across the room and vanished, and I was awakened by an indescribably sweet song of many voices. In that instant a certitude, which no words can express, came upon me that my mother had just died. And that was true. I was unable to understand the tremendous weight of the painful knowledge I received in advance, and wrote a letter to Sir William Crookes while still under the domination of these impressions and in poor bodily health. When I recovered I sought for a long time the external cause of this strange manifestation and, to my great relief, I succeeded after many months of fruitless effort. I had seen the painting of a celebrated artist, representing allegorically one of the seasons in the form of a cloud with a group of angels which seemed to actually float in the air, and this had struck me forcefully. It was exactly the same that appeared in my dream, with the exception of my mother's likeness. The music came from the choir in the church nearby at the early mass of Easter morning, explaining everything satisfactorily in conformity with scientific facts.

This occurred long ago, and I have never had the faintest reason since to change my views on psychical and spiritual phenomena, for which there is absolutely no foundation. The belief in these is the natural outgrowth of intellectual development. Religious dogmas are no longer accepted in their orthodox meaning, but every individual clings to faith in a supreme power of some kind. We all must have an ideal to govern our conduct and insure contentment, but it is immaterial whether it be one of creed, art, science or anything else, so long as it fulfills the function of a dematerializing force. It is essential to the peaceful existence of humanity as a whole that one common conception should prevail.

While I have failed to obtain any evidence in support of the contentions of psychologists and spiritualists, I have proved to my complete satisfaction the automatism of life, not only through continuous observations of individual actions, but even more conclusively through certain generalizations. These amount to a discovery which I consider of the greatest moment to human society, and on which I shall briefly dwell. I got the first inkling of this astounding truth when I was still a very young man, but for many years I interpreted what I noted simply as coincidences. Namely, whenever either myself or a person to whom I was attached, or a cause to which I was devoted, was hurt by others in a particular way, which might be best popularly characterized as the most unfair imaginable, I experienced a singular and undefinable pain which, for want of a better term, I have qualified as "cosmic," and shortly thereafter, and invariably, those who had inflicted it came to grief. After many such cases I confided this to a number of friends, who had the opportunity to convince themselves of the truth of the theory which I have gradually formulated and which may be stated in the following few words:

Our bodies are of similar construction and exposed to the same external influences. This results in likeness of response and concordance of the general activities on which all our social and other rules and laws are based. We are automata entirely controlled by the forces of the medium being tossed about like corks on the surface of the water, but mistaking the resultant of the impulses from the outside for free will. The movements and other actions we perform are always life preservative and tho seemingly quite independent from one another, we are connected by invisible links. So long as the organism is in perfect order it responds accurately to the agents that prompt it, but the moment that there is some derangement in any individual, his self-preservative power is impaired. Everybody understands, of course, that if one becomes deaf, has his eyesight weakened, or his limbs injured, the chances for his continued existence are lessened. But this is also true, and perhaps more so, of certain defects in the brain which deprive the automaton, more or less, of that vital quality and cause it to rush into destruction. A very sensitive and observant being, with his highly developed mechanism all intact, and acting with precision in obedience to the changing conditions of the environment, is endowed with a transcending mechanical sense, enabling him to evade perils too subtle to be directly perceived. When he comes in contact with others whose controlling organs are radically faulty, that sense asserts itself and he feels the "cosmic" pain. The truth of this has been borne out in hundreds of instances and I am inviting other students of nature to devote attention to this subject, believing that thru combined and systematic effort results of incalculable value to the world will be attained.

The idea of constructing an automaton, to bear out my theory, presented itself to me early but I did not begin active work until 1893, when I started my wireless investigations. During the succeeding two or three years a number of automatic mechanisms, to be actuated from a distance, were constructed by me and exhibited to visitors in my laboratory. In 1896, however, I designed a complete machine capable of a multitude of operations, but the consummation of my labors was delayed until late in 1897. This machine was illustrated and described in my article in the Century Magazine of June, 1900, and other periodicals of that time and, when first shown in the beginning of 1898, it created a sensation such as no other invention of mine has ever produced. In November, 1898, a basic patent on the novel art was granted to me, but only after the Examiner-in-Chief had come to New York and witnessed the performance, for what I claimed seemed unbelievable. I remember that when later I called on an official in Washington, with a view of offering the invention to the Government, he burst out in laughter upon my telling him what I had accomplished. Nobody thought then that there was the faintest prospect of perfecting such a device. It is unfortunate that in this patent, following the advice of my attorneys, I indicated the control as being effected thru the medium of a single circuit and a well-known form of detector, for the reason that I had not yet secured protection on my methods and apparatus for individualization. As a matter of fact, my boats were controlled thru the joint action of several circuits and interference of every kind was excluded. Most generally I employed receiving circuits in the form of loops, including condensers, because the discharges of my high-tension transmitter ionized the air in the hall so that even a very small aerial would draw electricity from the surrounding atmosphere for hours. Just to give an idea, I found, for instance, that a bulb $12''$ in diameter, highly exhausted, and with one single terminal to which a short wire was attached, would deliver well on to one thousand successive flashes before all charge of the air in the laboratory was neutralized. The loop form of receiver was not sensitive to such a disturbance and it is curious to note that it is becoming popular at this late date. In reality it collects much less energy than the aerials or a long grounded wire, but it so happens that it does away with a number of defects inherent to the present wireless devices. In demonstrating my invention before audiences, the visitors were requested to ask any questions, however involved, and the automaton would answer them by signs. This was considered magic at that time but was extremely simple, for it was myself who gave the replies by means of the device.

At the same period another larger telautomatic boat was constructed a photograph of which is shown in this number of the ELECTRICAL EXPERIMENTER. It was controlled by loops, having several turns placed in the hull, which was made entirely water-tight and capable of submergence. The apparatus was similar to that used in the first with the exception of certain special features I introduced as, for example, incandescent lamps which afforded a visible evidence of the proper functioning of the machine.

These automata, controlled within the range of vision of the operator, were, however, the first and rather crude steps in the evolution of the Art of Telautomatics as I had conceived it. The next logical improvement was its application to automatic mechanisms beyond the limits of vision and at great distance from the center of control, and I have ever since advocated their employment as instruments of warfare in preference to guns. The importance of this now seems to be recognized, if I am to judge from casual announcements thru the press of achievements which are said to be extraordinary but contain no merit of novelty, whatever. In an imperfect manner it is practicable, with the existing wireless plants, to launch an aeroplane, have it follow a certain approximate course, and perform some operation at a distance of many hundreds of miles. A machine of this kind can also be mechanically controlled in several ways and I have no doubt that it may prove of some usefulness in war. But there are, to my best knowledge, no instrumentalities in existence today with which such an object could be accomplished in a precise manner. I have devoted years of study to this matter and have evolved means, making such and greater wonders easily realizable.

As stated on a previous occasion, when I was a student at college I conceived a flying machine quite unlike the present ones. The underlying principle was sound but could not be carried into practice for want of a prime-mover of sufficiently great activity. In recent years I have successfully solved this problem and am now planning aerial machines devoid of sustaining planes, ailerons, propellers and other external attachments, which will be capable of immense speeds and are very likely to furnish powerful arguments for peace in the near future. Such a machine, sustained and propelled entirely by reaction, is supposed to be controlled either mechanically or by wireless energy. By installing proper plants it will be practicable to project a missile of this kind into the air and drop it almost on the very spot designated, which may be thousands of miles away. But we are not going to stop at this. Telautomata will be ultimately produced, capable of acting as if possessed of their own intelligence, and their advent will create a revolution. As early as 1898 I proposed to representatives of a large manufacturing concern the construction and public exhibition of an automobile carriage which, left to itself, would perform a great variety of operations involving something akin to judgment. But my proposal was deemed chimerical at that time and nothing came from it.

At present many of the ablest minds are trying to devise expedients for preventing a repetition of the awful conflict which is only theoretically ended and the duration and main issues of which I have correctly predicted in an article printed in the Sun of December 20,1914. The proposed League is not a remedy but on the contrary, in the opinion of a number of competent men, may bring about results just the opposite. It is particularly regrettable that a punitive policy was adopted in framing the terms of peace, because a few years hence it will be possible for nations to fight without armies, ships or guns, by weapons far more terrible, to the destructive action and range of which there is virtually no limit. A city, at any distance whatsoever from the enemy, can be destroyed by him and no power on earth can stop him from doing so. If we want to avert an impending calamity and a state of things which may transform this globe into an inferno, we should push the development of flying machines and wireless transmission of energy without an instant's delay and with all the power and resources of the nation.